ॐ▲

Contacts With The Gods From Space

Pathway to the New Age

GEORGE KING, D.D., TH.D.

WITH

RICHARD LAWRENCE, TH.D.

First Published—1996

Second Edition—2014

Contacts With The Gods From Space
Pathway to the New Age

www.aetherius.org

Manufactured in the United States of America.

Other books by George King, D.D., Th.D.

THE NINE FREEDOMS
THE DAY THE GODS CAME
THE TWELVE BLESSINGS
VISIT TO THE LOGOS OF EARTH
OPERATION SPACE MAGIC—THE COSMIC CONNECTION
OPERATION SPACE POWER—The Solution to the Spiritual Energy Crisis
CONTACT WITH A LORD OF KARMA
YOU TOO CAN HEAL
YOU ARE RESPONSIBLE!
THE THREE SAVIOURS ARE HERE!
THE FIVE TEMPLES OF GOD
THE AGE OF AETHERIUS
THE HOLY MOUNTAINS OF THE WORLD
OPERATION SUNBEAM—GOD'S MAGIC IN ACTION
WISDOM OF THE PLANETS
LIFE ON THE PLANETS
COSMIC VOICE, VOLUME NO. 1
COSMIC VOICE, VOLUME NO. 2
KARMA AND REINCARNATION
BECOME A BUILDER OF THE NEW AGE
THIS IS THE HOUR OF TRUTH
JOIN YOUR SHIP
A COSMIC MESSAGE OF DIVINE OPPORTUNITY
MY CONTACT WITH THE GREAT WHITE BROTHERHOOD
THE FESTIVAL OF "CARRYING THE LIGHT"
DESTRUCTION OF THE TEMPLE OF DEATH and RESCUE IN SPACE
JESUS COMES AGAIN
THE HEATHER ANGEL STORY
SPACE CONTACT IN SANTA BARBARA
THE ATOMIC MISSION
A SPECIAL ASSIGNMENT
CONTACT YOUR HIGHER SELF THROUGH YOGA
BOOK OF SACRED PRAYERS
THE PRACTICES OF AETHERIUS
THE FLYING SAUCERS
THE TRUTH ABOUT DYNAMIC PRAYER
IMPORTANCE OF COMMEMORATION and SPIRITUAL HAPPINESS
A SERIES OF LESSONS ON SPIRITUAL SCIENCE ON CD

By George King, D.D., Th.D. with Richard Lawrence, Th.D.
REALISE YOUR INNER POTENTIAL

By Richard Lawrence,
THE MAGIC OF HEALING
Published by Mind Body Spirit Direct
GODS, GUIDES AND GUARDIAN ANGELS (with Mark Bennett)
Published by O Books
UNLOCK YOUR PSYCHIC POWERS
Published by O Books
PRAYER ENERGY (with Mark Bennett)
Published by CICO Books
UFOS AND THE EXTRATERRESTRIAL MESSAGE
Published by CICO Books

Books, CDs and DVDs by George King, D.D., Th.D. and Richard
Lawrence, are obtainable from The Aetherius Society, American
Headquarters, 6202 Afton Place, Hollywood, California 90028, U.S.A.,
Tel: (323) 465-9652 or (323) 467-HEAL; or from the European
Headquarters of The Aetherius Society, 757 Fulham Road, London SW6
5UU, England, Tel: (020) 7736-4187. www.aetherius.org

Cover design and illustration by Rodney D. Crosby.

DEDICATION

This book is dedicated to
our Cosmic Saviours
Who have watched over us
through the centuries.

Contents

Illustrations

Dr. George King receiving a Cosmic Transmission

Foreword to the Second Edition

In the Summer of 1995 I was staying with Dr. George King at his home in Santa Barbara, California. One day, out of the blue, he turned to me and said: "you seem very prolific—why don't you write a book with me?"

I had written two books, one of which had been declared by its publisher to be an international best-seller. But, that amounted to nothing when compared to the body of works published by Dr. King, which will surely go down in history as classics of new age metaphysics. The thought, never mind the privilege, of co-authoring a book with Dr. King had never occurred to me until he spoke those words.

And so was born *Contacts With The Gods From Space*, which turned out to be the last book by Dr. King to be published in his lifetime. With the advice of International Directors of The Aetherius Society from London and Los Angeles, the synopsis of the book was developed, the manuscript completed and approved by Dr. King and it was launched at London's Festival for Mind Body Spirit in May 1996.

For the next year a major promotional campaign ensued involving talks in dozens of towns and cities in the U.K., U.S.A., Canada, Australia and New Zealand. In the U.K. the first lecture in Leicester was heralded by a widely reported UFO sighting just two hours before the lecture, and the last in Torquay was preceded by a headline in the local press on the day of the meeting that a UFO had been seen heading for Torbay. Neither report was made by anyone connected to our campaign, but it is not unusual for such "synchronicity" to occur when promoting the cosmic message.

The campaign was a triumphant success, enthusiastically supported and encouraged by phone calls and faxes from Dr. King who, in view of his health and other commitments, could not participate physically. One such fax sent to us in London simply read: "Your current Campaign in the British Isles is: WONDERFUL! WONDERFUL!! WONDERFUL!!! WONDER-FUL!!!! WONDERFUL!!!!! I send my most sincere Blessings to all those concerned in this magnificent Campaign."

In a matter of months, it was necessary for the book to be reprinted with sufficient stocks for the future. These have now finally run out and this second edition has been published with the agreement of the Board of International Directors of The Aetherius Society. I should add that neither Dr. King nor I have taken royalties from this book, nor will I ever do so.

Much has changed since 1995, especially in the field of scientific research, but the timeless Truths remain the same. The subtitle has been changed from "Pathway to the New Millennium" to "Pathway to the New Age", since, prior to the year 2000 "new millennium" was often used to indicate "new age", which is no longer the case. There are a few minor edits, but the text is essentially exactly as it was in 1996.

On July 12th, 1997, Dr. King passed from this earthly realm at his residence in Santa Barbara. When this book was launched, Dr. King asked me to convey his blessings to readers and now, as it enters its second edition, I am honoured to do so again.

Dr. Richard Lawrence

Preface

The latter part of the second millennium A.D., has seen an abundance of metaphysical knowledge of all kinds being made available, for the first time, to humanity as a whole. Numerous Sanskrit texts have been translated into modern languages, often deciphered from obscure, codified systems into understandable, practical philosophies. The Theosophical movement, originally led by the much maligned but inspired Madame H.P. Blavatsky, has produced a wealth of complex but invaluable revelations from the Spiritual Hierarchy of Earth (the Great White Brotherhood). The doors of western mystery schools have been opened to reveal advanced magical rituals based on natural forces. Yogis and mystics have left India, Tibet and other parts of the world to visit the west and teach hitherto unknown practices in higher consciousness and Spiritual transformation.

At the same time as this ancient, formerly secret knowledge has become available to the world as a whole, an apparently new phenomenon has also emerged, namely UFO's (Unidentified Flying Objects). On June 24th, 1947, Kenneth Arnold, when flying his private plane in Washington State, U.S.A., saw nine disc-shaped objects in the sky which he described as being like saucers skipping over water. The term "Flying Saucer" was coined, and so the UFO movement was born. Nowadays, any informed person is aware of this phenomenon and knows something about it. No longer is it regarded as an eccentric belief, but rather as a perfectly logical and consistent recognition of a phenomenon which has been with us throughout history.

Into this maelstrom of philosophical change stepped Dr. George King. Born on January 23rd, 1919, he was to combine a mastery of the mystical and Yogic sciences, which he had attained by a highly disciplined regime of intense practice in the ten years after the Second World War, with a unique series of close encounters with extraterrestrial sources spanning over 40 years. In his person, this movement of ancient knowledge from east to west and from secret ashrams to modern bookshops, was to take on a new, Cosmic dimension. In 1955, The Aetherius Society was formed to propagate the Flying Saucer message as delivered by and through Dr. George King.

Nowadays, it is fairly commonplace to hear of claimed close encounters with UFO's. The shelves of bookshops around the world display a whole variety of supposed messages from all over the Galaxy and beyond. So-called UFO abductions are being studied in universities and former government officials, who had previously discounted UFO claims, have changed their approach and, in one case, even written a book advocating their existence. Most people, according to opinion polls, believe in life on other Planets. It is not so much whether they exist, but who can you believe? Sadly, there have been fakes, hoaxers and, to be frank, deluded people who have misled others. But there have also been a few genuine UFO contactees. Of these, Dr. George King stands head and shoulders above all the other modern day contactees. There is simply no one to compare with him. Independent researchers have stated categorically that there is no organization in the world like The Aetherius Society, which has remained consistent in its beliefs over a period of over 40 years, has steadily grown into a highly respected, international organization and, above all, offers proof of its claims.

That is why I was delighted to be invited by Dr. King to co-author this book with him. In my view, he has written the most advanced and important works of metaphysical teaching available in modern literature. They provide the key to understanding the New Age and how to build it. They are written in easily understandable English, and yet go into uncharted territory of practical, mystical thought. Despite this and probably because they deal with such advanced Cosmic concepts, none of these books could be described as introductory or giving a broad overview of The Aetherius Society's work and philosophy, which has continually evolved up to and including the present day.

This book is based entirely upon Dr. King's contacts and personal wisdom as a Master of Yoga in his own right. I have written the book as a result of over 20 years as his student and friend and the many discussions we have had. I will also include excerpts from his lectures and writings throughout the book. Additionally, extracts from some of the numerous messages he has received from extraterrestrial sources will be included. In short, the concept of the book is his—the overall format we have agreed together—the writing is mine.

If you are wondering what exactly The Aetherius Society is, I hope you will find your answer here. If you want to know the Spiritual aspect of the UFO phenomenon and to come into contact with the most outstanding series of close encounters with Interplanetary Beings in modern times, then you will do so in this book. I am not out to convert you to anything. That would be a futile exercise. I know that if you are interested in what I say, you will investigate for yourself. I also know that if you do so, you will find your own proof in your own way. I invite you to examine all the facts and test all the claims you will read about for yourself. I believe that if you do, it will be the most profitable thing you have ever done. At least that is what I found twenty-four years ago when I first came across The Aetherius Society.

Dr. Richard Lawrence

CHAPTER ONE

Science and Religion

"Science, by itself, is like the soul-less wanderer of the realms of night."

— *the Master Jesus.*

HISTORICAL ROOTS

At one time in ancient Greece, there were no divisions between science and religion. Both were seen as essential aspects of the only real study: the search for Truth. Sharp divisions were not made then, as they are now, between the physical world and the Spiritual world. They were both seen as parts of one great whole. Their educational system encouraged a breadth of learning, in which, for example, mathematics, music and astronomy were seen as being interrelated, since there are parallels between the harmony of numbers, sounds and celestial bodies. All studies were only stepping stones for the student to move onto the most important fields of, first philosophy and then, the even higher field of theology.

In the ancient east, science and religion were also seen as coming from the same root—that of Yoga, which means "Union with God." Those ancient Yogis, known in the Hindu Vedas as Rishis, applied their brilliant powers of scientific analysis to the internal human condition in order to develop a workable system of personal Spiritual evolution. From this sprang the great eastern wisdom which was written down thousands of years later by Vedic scribes and has never been more accessible than it is today.

Gradually through the centuries, science has become separated from religion. The scientific discoveries made since the

Renaissance have changed our whole concept of the Universe. Our knowledge of the physical world has been revolutionized in comparison with the relatively superstitious beliefs of the middle ages. We have felt the benefits of this in too many fields to enumerate, from transport to medicine to communication to construction and so on. But we have also seen the indiscriminate development of science for warfare and we are faced with a threat that the people of the middle ages never faced: that of complete obliteration through a nuclear holocaust. Science has been developed too much for its own sake, instead of purely for humanitarian purposes. The nightmare scenario has occurred. Science when used for atomic warfare is indeed the "soul-less wanderer of the realms of night."

Religion cannot escape its share of the blame. Divisions have permeated the world religions, both between religions and within the religions themselves. How many wars have been fought between different sects of the same religion, never mind different religions? And yet, the basic tenets of all the major religions are similar in essence. They each gave their own individual emphasis for the time and place in which they emerged, but it is amazing just how much they all have in common. Buddhism sprang out of Hinduism and the Christian and Moslem faiths have their roots in Judaism. The Old Testament itself shares common ground with Hinduism. For example, the God of Abraham is referred to as "I Am That I Am," which is very close to a translation of an ancient Mantra contained in Sanskrit writings, and used for centuries by both Hindus and Buddhists.

SCIENCE IN THE NEW AGE

A time of change is now upon us. The Age of Aquarius, which will start to dawn in the new millennium, will be an Age of science, but a science tempered by love. The barriers between different religions will gradually be broken down and there will be a return to oneness which is the very essence of Spiritual expression. More than this, the barriers between religion and science will be broken down and they will be seen again as two essential aspects of the one search for Truth.

If you consider this concept impossibly optimistic, just look at the massive changes which have occurred in our perception of the Universe in a few hundred years. From the time of Aristotle in the 4th century B.C., until the theories of Copernicus in the 16th century A.D., the Universe was considered by scientists and theologians alike to be entirely centred around the Earth. There was a virtual lone voice in the 3rd century B.C., namely the Alexandrian astronomer Aristarchus of Samos, who boldly maintained that the Earth moved around the Sun. But it was 1800 years before the visionary findings of this inspired individual were confirmed by Copernicus, Galileo and others. This proves absolutely that the view held by the religious and scientific establishments of the day, and often the vast majority of thinking people, is not necessarily correct. Even in the 16th century, when Galileo supported the Copernican findings that the Earth was not the centre of the Universe, it was too much for the establishment to stomach and he was forced to recant after appalling treatment at the hands of the Catholic Church.

Albert Einstein compared scientific discoveries to looking at a watch. You can observe the movement of a watch and deduce from that how it may work, but you will only ultimately know by removing the back of the watch and looking inside. Scientists, he said, have not looked inside, they are only making deductions based upon looking at the watch. After 1800 years of science accepting the Aristotelian concept that Planets were embedded in a crystalline sphere which moved in a uniform circular motion around the Earth, scientists such as Galileo, Newton and Kepler started to understand concepts of planetary motion, the laws of gravity and so on. Once their discoveries were accepted, so the religious and scientific establishments and the views of most thinking people changed.

Dr. George King could be likened to Aristarchus of Samos in being centuries ahead of his time. As with Aristarchus, orthodoxy has rejected his views, but a change will come as it always does. The New Age will see science and religion draw closer together and the Spiritual Sciences, now being championed by Dr. King and a few others, will eventually emerge as the established approach of the Aquarian Age. This time it should not take 1800 years though.

As scientists have moved into studying the minutiae of sub-atomic physics, they have found that the predictable fixed laws which they had come to assume were universal to all matter, no longer apply at the sub-atomic level. This discovery in the early years of the 20th century shook the very foundations of physics. Sub-atomic particles were not behaving as they should do. Since the Greek philosopher and scientist Democritus, who lived in the 5th century B.C., had introduced the concept of atoms and space as the only certain elements in the physical world, up to the discoveries of Sir Isaac Newton and the Newtonian physicists who followed him, a vision of a perfectly ordered Universe which conformed to known laws and never deviated from them had evolved. Suddenly in the 20th century came the discovery that sub-atomic particles appeared to behave haphazardly.

Despite the apparently haphazard behaviour of particles of matter, they nevertheless cooperated with the Newtonian laws of physics when acting in combination together, which raised a very fundamental question. Why should they cooperate en masse with the laws of wave motion, gravity and so on, if there is no predictable law governing the behaviour of an individual particle? What force causes them in combination to work predictably and perfectly, when they do not do so when analyzed individually? This paradox has perplexed the theoretical physicists of the 20th century.

Other startling facts have also come to light recently. Biophysicists are staggered by what their research tells them about the Planet on which we live. The apparently coincidental composition of the atmosphere of Earth, which had succeeded in keeping surface temperatures constant despite the unpredictable effects of Sun and time, made it look more like an artifact than an accident—something created and maintained by a higher Power.

Increased scientific knowledge was pointing inexorably towards a force beyond matter guiding and controlling the function of the Universe. Scientists have stated that we do not know why natural qualities, such as the strength of gravity, the speed of light, the electrical charge on the electron and so on have the values they do. They point to the fact that the slightest variation of their values would result in a barren Universe without Stars or light and question why they are so precisely adjusted as to give rise to life. Questions such as these indicate a religious dimension to science—the two are no longer separable.

LIFE ON OTHER PLANETS

It is now generally accepted that the likelihood of life on other Planets is overwhelming. Scientists speculate that the odds of no Planets existing in the Cosmos which could sustain physical life as we know it on Earth are minuscule. Current estimates are that there are 400,000,000,000 Suns in the Milky Way Galaxy, and that conservatively at least one out of ten of these Stars is orbited by Planets—in other words, has its own Solar System. Assuming that each of these Solar Systems contains approximately ten Planets, there are at least 400,000,000,000 Planets in this Galaxy alone. These Planets may also be orbited by large satellites which are capable of sustaining physical life as we know it. If one in a hundred of these Planets or satellites is physically habitable, there would be billions of them which could support organic existence.

But this only deals with physical life as we know it; it does not deal with higher vibratory realms of existence. As science and religion come closer in the Aquarian Age, the existence of higher frequencies of matter will be seriously examined. What is the soul, for example, and on what frequency level does it exist? What is the astral body which so many have experienced in near death and out of body experiences? What exactly happens when you die and where do you go? Metaphysicians believe that all life is contained in a sea of energy which vibrates at different levels. There are many realms around this Earth, all dovetailed into each other and by understanding the concept of higher frequencies of matter, all these questions can be answered. This is arguably the most important step for science to take in the New Age.

Once you accept that there are many realms of existence around this Earth, new possibilities are opened up for the Universe as a whole. You start to see the whole Cosmos as being permeated by energy levels of existence. Ideas like this are not new—other planetary realms are referred to in Buddhist writings, for example, as "lokas" (heavenly spheres). But they need to be taken out of the domain of purely religious belief and into the field of practical experience. Beliefs are, of course, essential to all of us. We all have them, not least the dedicated skeptic who can be the most dogmatic individual of all. But the amalgamation of religion and science will bring the application of belief to experience and hence produce knowledge.

There are higher frequency levels of existence not only on this Earth, but also on Mars, Jupiter, Venus, Saturn and other Planets within this Solar System and throughout the Galaxies. Space probes to other Planets in this Solar System will only discover what they are permitted to discover by the inhabitants of those worlds. They do not use the same basic frequency of physical existence as us, since they vibrate at higher rates caused by their greater Spiritual advancement. Their science includes the ability to travel through the levels—they have a control over different frequencies of energy which causes them to be invisible on this level. This explains the ability of UFO's to disappear and re-appear, a phenomenon which has been reported by thousands of people around the world. UFO's have often been described as virtually blinking in and out of existence.

THE NATURE OF THE UNIVERSE

Current science says that the Universe will always expand. Scientists believe that billions of years ago the Universe contained matter and energy of extraordinarily high density and temperature which exploded in the so-called "big bang." As the gas expanded and cooled, protons and neutrons were formed, and some of these built helium nuclei. Eventually, complete hydrogen and helium atoms formed; the gas condensed into Galaxy-sized clouds which broke up into Stars. Contrary to the views of earlier astronomers that Stars were tranquil and unchanging, it is now believed that they are born, lead violent lives and die. After the last Star has faded, scientists believe that even protons may decay into much lighter particles and the Universe may end as a sea of electrons, neutrons and forms of radiation.

This idea of creation, followed by expansion, followed by dissolution is the very essence of not only modern physics, but also ancient Yoga philosophy. The yogis depict it in the following way: Out of Potential came the "Outbreathing," which brought about Creation and Manifestation. This was followed by the "Inbreathing," which dissolved Creation and returned Manifestation back to Potential again. As science advances, so it returns inevitably to fundamental religious concepts. Many studies have been made of the remarkable parallels in thinking between eastern wisdom and modern physics.

We are familiar from science fiction with the concept of "black holes" in Space. These are considered to be collapsed Stars which have shrunk to minute sizes due to the phenomenal gravitational forces upon their mass. Scientists describe a "black hole" as an ultra-dense cauldron of matter and energy which has such gravitational force that even light cannot escape from its vicinity. They theorize that "black holes" will gradually absorb other matter within their gravitational fields, drawing Stars and Planets gradually into their frozen interiors and bringing about an absorption of the Universe as a whole.

As scientific models have been drawn up to calculate the structure of the Universe, theoretical physicists have discovered that, according to the known laws of gravity, there is not enough mass present in the Universe to hold Galaxies together. They should theoretically be separating apart from each other because there is not enough mass to exert sufficient gravitational force to hold them together. To explain this, they postulate that the force must be exerted by "dark matter". This assumption raises several questions, the most fundamental of which is whether our understanding of the laws of gravity in Space is complete enough to make such a deduction in the first place. But it also indicates that there is some kind of force at work at the macrocosmic level, just as sub-atomic physicists found at the microcosmic level, which is keeping in being the Universe as we know it. Something is causing the Galaxies to hold together, just as something is causing particles to cooperate with the natural law of physics. Even if it is "dark matter," as physicists speculate, it is exactly the right amount to achieve the balance required throughout the Cosmos. Too much, they say, would have caused disintegration through the absorption of planetary bodies into "black holes," and too little would have caused the separation of Galaxies leading to unknown consequences. The more science makes progress, the closer it moves towards religion.

TIME TRAVEL

During the mid-1980's, theoretical physicists turned to the

possibility of the existence of "Cosmic worm holes." These would be interstellar passageways through which it would be possible to travel to another part of the Galaxy and even another part of the Universe in a very short space of time. In fact, an increasing number of scientists believe that through a "Cosmic worm hole," time travel would be possible. As fanciful as this may sound, it has gone way beyond the realm of science fiction and is now being studied very seriously in universities around the world.

The fact that time is the fourth dimension and only exists relative to velocity has been proved many times. In 1972, four of the most accurate atomic clocks available were put on board an aircraft and flown around the world. They were flown each way, east and west. At the end of the trip they were found to be slightly behind their stationary earthbound counterparts with which they were synchronized before the flight. This proved that time slows down at velocities relative to a stationary point. Through a combination of exceptional physical forces, many theoretical physicists now regard time travel as a possibility. For time travel to take place, there must be some kind of distortion in the parameters of Space and gravity. After all, we measure time in terms of the movement of bodies in Space which are governed by fixed gravitational fields, e.g. the Earth revolving round the Sun. Such a distortion could be caused by the existence of so-called "Cosmic worm holes," which would be even more extreme combinations of mass, energy and gravity than a "black hole."

Of course, all this is pure hypothesis and based upon certain preconceptions which may well turn out to be wrong. One such preconception which is being increasingly rejected is the fact that the speed of light is the ultimate velocity. Physics is moving into metaphysical territory. The two can no longer be completely separated. Time travel raises moral issues. If you can theoretically alter your past or future by time travel, what

effect would that have on your present? If you can travel for-
wards or backwards in time, do you retain all the knowledge
you currently have and how does this affect your capacity to
experience? And so on. If you deal with such concepts, you
have automatically moved into the sphere of metaphysics and
religion.

Much of the current thinking in science was foreshadowed
by an outstanding experience enjoyed by Dr. George King on
December 6th, 1957. Of all the close encounters with extraterrestrial Intelligences which have been recorded in history, this
will rank as one of the most significant in changing the parameters of future scientific and metaphysical thought. The following description of this amazing happening, in which he visited a Satellite from Mars, is related in the words of Dr. George
King.

A CLOSE ENCOUNTER IN SPACE

"I entered the shield of invisibility surrounding
the Vessel. This invisibility is caused by the rotation
of photons in a 360 degree arc on the fringe of the
magnetic protective shield itself. Then a thin green-
ish ray, hollow inside, formed a magnetic tunnel
through the protective force shield, through which I
entered the Satellite.

"The Operations Room was the same as I had seen
it in a previous visit. This time a purple glow filled
the large semi-circular room. I could see the great
flawless crystal window, which extended over one
quarter of the ceiling surface, was charged by violet
coloured energies. These energies impose whatever
conditioning is desired by the operators of the
Satellite upon the Solar rays which flow through the
large crystal window. The three great prismatic crystals beneath the window transmitted the energy into

a large, egg-shaped crystal in the middle of the semi-circular floor. This crystal seemed to glow with an inner fire as did the multi-shaped ones which floated around it like miniature Planets silently moving around a central, oval-shaped Sun. In turn, the vibrations produced, by the reaction of this specially prepared Solar energy upon the other crystal formations, were projected into the series of transmitting crystals and from there to every life-stream on Earth who needed and used this Spiritual Energy.

"A wonderful perfume filled the air, seeming to caress my subtle body and imparting a gentle stimulation which heightened my awareness.

"The Martian whom I had met previously, smiled in greeting. His golden-brown skin—completely hairless—was without a wrinkle. I already knew his age to be over 300 years and marvelled at his youthful appearance.

"The Martian picked up my thoughts and smilingly answered, 'Control of mind, my friend, brings as one of its inevitable results the control of matter.'

"I noticed that this time he wore a wide belt, studded with jewel-like crystals, over his one-piece, tightly fitting suit.

"'Come,' invited the Martian, as he led the way across the Operations Room towards an aperture in the opposite wall between two banks of dials and rows of different coloured push-buttons.

"We entered a short tunnel about seven feet high and five feet across. This was illuminated by concealed lighting which threw a diffused but shadowless pink glow upon the walls and floor. The pink glow exerted a steadying influence upon my auric bodies and became absorbed into them, thus causing a swift movement of the molecules which sounded like a high pitched trilling noise, as molecule rubbed against molecule. I could feel a gently stimulating warm tingle throughout my whole structure. A most pleasant and refreshing feeling.

"The tunnel ended abruptly and I was led into a long, low, oblong-shaped room. Upon the walls were what appeared to me to be maps and charts of Constellations and Galaxies. Many symbols unknown to me appeared here and there as though to pinpoint the different Star systems. Each Sun radiated its own particular colour changes, as did the clusters of Planets which surrounded that Sun. The Planets in the Solar System were also shown as large, glowing balls of colour with their attendant satellites, some lighted by the reflected rays of the Sun revolving around them. A complete chart of the Heavens in moving picture form, took up the full length of the walls of the room. I marvelled at the wonder of the magnificent pictures of the Heavens.

"Why, they are three dimensional!

"'No, my dear friend. These charts are at least seven dimensional,' telepathed the Martian. 'As you already know, the fourth dimension is time. If you regard those projections with care you can denote certain changes taking place, which are caused by the movement of the satellites around their Suns and so on. Such basic changes are accurately predictable, therefore these changes take place within a measurable time sequence. Now, manifestation could not exist without a power which is capable of creating the tension necessary to hold the particles of matter in a certain state which constitutes the nucleus of sub-atomic and atomic structure. This power utilizes energy and is capable of imposing certain limits upon the energy of motion. The power which imposes direction upon motion is—mind! Now, mind by itself is an all-pervasive energy which, for the sake of simplicity, you could term as a pattern of potential. A pattern which to all intents is static until pressures are applied from outside, which dictate direction to it. *Therefore, even basic matter exists within this framework. Will, Mind, Motion, Time, Length, Breadth and Height.* The Divine Will imposes those conditions upon mind which bring its potential into manifestation as directed motion in a time-frame of length, breadth and height. Of course this is but a simplified version of a profound concept, as you no doubt see. Divine Will cannot *Itself* be measured, for It is above and beyond its own manifestations, but we do have some idea of the basic function of this Power. There are even "sub" states, such as feeling, which I have purposely avoided in order to simplify your explanation of the subject.'

"'Thank you for that!' I spluttered. 'It's going to be difficult enough to put that much over.'

"'I have no doubt that you will find a way,' replied the Martian, with a twinkle in his blue eyes.

"He spoke with such an easy grace about a subject which has baffled some of Earth's most profound thinkers, that it seemed easy for me to understand him while I was in his presence. I can now only hope that I have done his explanation the justice it undoubtedly deserves."

SEVEN DIMENSIONS OF CREATION

This staggering but simply expressed summation of the dimensions in which all life exists will become the basis of the science of the future. Scientists realize today that the mind of the researcher can have a definite effect on the outcome of an experiment. No longer are they able to apply the principle of physical objectivity as the only means of proof, an idea which dominated scientific thinking for so long. Length, breadth, height and time are generally accepted as the first four dimensions. Since time exists only in relation to velocity, it is becoming gradually clear to thinking people that, as this great Martian revealed to Dr. King, the fifth dimension must be motion. The next step for scientists to realize is that the sixth dimension is mind. Once they have grasped this they will see that behind the behaviour of even celestial objects there is another power at work operating through mind-controlled energy. This controlling force is the seventh dimension: Divine Will. Call it God, Brahma, Allah, Jehovah, Great White Spirit, or by any other name, it is Divine Will operating through mind. When science realizes this, it will have moved firmly into the territory of religion. There will be a return, certainly much the wiser, to the old idea of the ancient Greeks that the highest study of all must be theology, the study of the God- given laws of the Universe.

This can all be summarized in a simple but profound aphorism stated by Dr. George King:

> **"There is no science without religion and no religion without science."**

It will no longer be good enough in the New Age for religions to hide behind the concept of a "leap of faith." Certainly faith is essential in all major endeavours, but it is not good enough when asked a searching question to merely call for a leap of faith. Any religion worth its salt can be tested. The fact that the Roman Catholic Church in the 17th century was not able to accept the scientific findings of Copernicus and Galileo was an indictment of that religion at the time. By the same token, in these days, all religious organizations should be able to explain the existence of UFO's, what exactly happens when you die, the meaning of parapsychological events and so on.

The quotation which headed this chapter was delivered by the Master Jesus through Dr. King in Samadhic trance at the Caxton Hall in London on September 14th, 1957. The full statement made by this Great Master at that time encapsulates many of the points made in this chapter. You are recommended to use it as a meditation, for if you do, you will gain a profound and lasting realization from it:

"The Age which is breaking now, brings with it great possibilities and is the Age of Science. Science, by itself, is like the soul-less wanderer of the realms of night. Yet a warmth will come out of Love, to fashion it into a tool, so that it becometh as a wise man, finding his home. Warm it with that Love, my brothers. Let that wondrous, everlasting Power from your hearts fall upon this Science, so that it becometh as a tool in the hands of Everlasting Divinity, and not that soul-less thing which you have made of it."

CHAPTER TWO

A Master for the Aquarian Age

"Judge a man by results."
— *Mars Sector 6*

CLOSE ENCOUNTERS IN HISTORY

There is an illogical tendency among some people to assume that all truly great, miraculous events happened in the past, but could not possibly happen now. Such people think that the Bible, Hindu scripts, Greek legends, Celtic myths and so on, are one thing, but nothing like this is ever going to happen in their lifetime. This view is all the more absurd when you consider the exceptional times in which we live. We now have the capacity for mass salvation or destruction. We have the potential either for diabolical warfare or to build a new world of peace and brotherhood. Despite this, there are still many who meticulously scour over ancient texts for signs of Divine Intervention, but blatantly refuse to believe in such things happening in these days.

One example of extraordinary Divine Intervention is the close encounters which have occurred with Dr. George King. He has a unique record of extraterrestrial contacts and has demonstrated it beyond doubt. But just because he is contemporary, some refuse point blank to accept his claims. They may seem strange, unlikely and even preposterous to some, but those are emotional reactions and have no bearing on whether they are true. The Teachings of Jesus were regarded in the same way by the Romans and many Jews, but are now the beliefs of hundreds of millions, including many who would not describe themselves as Christians.

Why should the great Spiritual happenings of man's history be confined to the past? Common sense suggests that, in this age of Space travel, mass communication and more potential for good or evil than ever in the past, such Spiritual events should be more frequent in these days, not less. There is nothing surprising in the fact that Intelligences from other Planets, who have been in contact with individuals on Earth throughout our history, should choose this time to make such an important series of contacts with an apparently ordinary man.

A popular myth is that UFO's are a new phenomenon. They are not. UFO's have been with us throughout history. They are referred to in the most ancient documents on Earth and have, significantly enough, often been connected with religious activity. Before looking at the claims and the evidence of Dr. King's contacts with Interplanetary Beings, it is important to put them into the right context—the context of a history of cooperation with people on this Planet by advanced Spiritual Intelligences from other worlds.

This is not a UFO book per se, both because there are numerous books already available on this subject, and also because the most important and unique aspect of the contacts of Dr. King are the close encounters with the inhabitants of other worlds which he has experienced, not so much their craft. However, it would be as well to describe briefly some of the revelations which have been made to Dr. King about extraterrestrial Spacecraft by their controllers.

Two of the most commonly sighted UFO's have consistently been the cigar-shaped object (Mother-Ship) and the so-called "Flying Saucer" (Scout Patrol Vessel). Both these types are reported in ancient records and many other sources up to the present day. The following information compiled by Dr. King, after receiving many contacts, offers a very useful guideline about these types of craft. Many of the points also apply to UFO's of other shapes and sizes.

MOTHER-SHIPS

These are shaped like cigars, fairly blunt at both ends. They vary in size from 1,000 yards to 5,000 miles in length. The small ones carry seven to nine Scout Patrol Vessels; the large ones up to 7,000 Scout Patrol Vessels. The very large ones make deep Space probes outside our System into Galaxies beyond. The Mother-Ships come to within 500 miles of Earth. Sometimes, according to the position of the Moon and magnetic forces emanating from the Sun, they approach nearer to the Earth's surface than that.

They are propelled by a magnetic device which exerts an equal thrust upon every atom of substance within the ship, thereby cancelling out any effects of gravitational weight which may be caused by high acceleration within the gravitational pull of a planetary body. The Carrier Vessels are made of organic metal which is susceptible to a concentration of thought waves emanated by their operators. This substance is thought to be self-reproducing. They are protected by a force field which is intensified in direct relation to the velocity of the craft. This force field is magnetic in nature and it causes a compass needle to oscillate and has a pronounced effect upon radio reception. The degree of this radio interference is determined by the intensity of the force field (i.e., the velocity of the Mother-Ship), as well as the position of the radio apparatus and shape of the aerial. This force field reflects and refracts light and causes a fuzzy effect on photographic plates. These radiations are not harmful to Earth people unless they come very near to a Mother-Ship in motion, that is, to within the outer edge of the force field itself. Obviously, no material body could actually come into contact with the hull of the vessel, while the force field is in operation. The force field protects the vessel and the occupants from atmospheric friction while travelling near to a planetary body, counteracting the otherwise disastrous effects which could be caused by severe magnetic fluctuations which are contacted while passing through the terrestrial ionospheric and heavy side layers, at the extremely high velocity of which these craft are capable.

SCOUT PATROL VESSELS

There are many types of Scout Patrol Vessels. The ones most often seen in the skies of the world are circular vessels with a dome on top, looking rather like an up-turned saucer, with half a smallish ball on top. There are four major types of this kind of craft, which vary in size and shape in keeping with the particular job on which they are engaged. Some of the large Flying Saucers carry a crew of five and others a crew of four. The most commonly used vessel carries a crew of two, with extra accommodation for several passengers if required. It has a diameter of 35 ft. 6 inches. The remote controlled vessels, for certain kinds of freighter usage, seem to be more bell-shaped, having a small flange at the bottom.

All these vessels have magnetic propulsion units and are protected by smaller editions of the same type of force screens which protect the Mother-Ships. The propulsion units of these craft are so designed as to be able to attract the great tides of energy which flow freely through the ether, which is wrongly called "empty space." The attraction of the power from these energy tides produces a reaction, i.e. energetic release. The forces so generated are controlled and are used for the motive power of these vessels.

The system of control of the natural fields of magnetic energy enables the operators of Scout Patrol Vessels to use the energy potential of existing gravitational fields, which may be used as a secondary propulsion unit, to enable easy landings on to and ascents from any planetary mass. They know that gravity is a dual-poled magnetic force and they are able to reverse these poles at will.

Some of these craft have been seen to perform a reciprocal

pattern of flight at fantastic speeds. Such aerobatics would only be possible if the force of gravity were known and controlled.

Some vessels from Interplanetary Parliament can be dematerialized at will by their operators and the vibratory octave of their existence so changed as to become invisible to our eyesight. This phenomenon has been noted on certain occasions by aircraft which have been pursuing these Flying Saucers.

Invisibility can also be brought about in another way. At times the operators of Scout Patrol Vessels and Mother-Ships choose to rotate the streams of photons around their craft in a 360° arc, thereby rendering themselves invisible to the ordinary eye.

ANCIENT RECORDS

According to the Roman poet Catullus, who lived from approximately 87 to 54 B.C., the writings of Homer refer to a time when the Gods from Space dwelt among the heroes of old. As he said in his Poem 64:

"For then, before religion was despised,
The Sky-dwellers in person used to visit
The stainless homes of heroes and be seen
At mortal gatherings."

There are many references in a variety of native tribal groups from different parts of the globe who had contact with and belief in advanced Beings from other worlds. But probably the two most accessible ancient sources which show these contacts in a religious context are the Holy Bible, which could virtually be described as a UFO compendium, and some of the Hindu texts.

THE HOLY BIBLE

The Bible is not completely accurate as an historical document. Numerous scholarly researchers have shown that not only has it been through different translations, but several different scribes have worked on it, some with political motivations of varying kinds, thereby introducing considerable potential for inconsistency. This does not make it worthless—far from it. It is a very valuable document, but it cannot be regarded as completely accurate. Everything which follows in this section should be read in the light of this.

The most often quoted account of a Biblical UFO occurs in the book of Ezekiel. This description, which is dated by scholars as occurring in approximately 600 B.C., took place when Ezekiel was among the captives in Chaldea by the Chebar River. Ezekiel, Chapter One, Verse Four, reads as follows:

"And I looked, and, and, behold, a whirlwind came out of the north, a great cloud, and a fire infolding itself, and a brightness was about it, and out of the midst thereof as the colour of amber, out of the midst of the fire."

This beautiful description of a UFO continues with what is commonly described as "a close encounter of the third kind." A close encounter of the first kind is a UFO sighting. This type of close encounter has been reported by hundreds of thousands of people around the world. A close encounter of the second kind includes some kind of physical evidence of a UFO sighting, such as a photograph or some physical substance from the craft. This type of close encounter is much rarer than the first, but there have been photographs taken of extraterrestrial Spacecraft. A close encounter of the third kind is a meeting with one or more occupants of UFO's who are visitors from other Planets. After studying the abundance of evidence for UFO's, there is no doubt that UFO's do exist and have been seen through the ages in a multitude of different countries and cultures. What many people do not realize is that according to opinion polls, believers in UFO's are in a majority, not a minority, as the media often like to imply.

The important thing about UFO's is not so much the craft itself, but the people who man and control these craft. Ezekiel's account is therefore very revealing. He witnessed four Interplanetary Beings stepping out of this UFO and received information and instructions from them. He referred to them as "living creatures." Later in the same chapter, there is a more detailed description of the Spacecraft which is described as "a wheel in the middle of a wheel" and having "eyes round about them four." This last description is taken to refer to portholes which have often been seen in UFO sightings. A wheel within a wheel could be an inner superstructure revolving whilst an outer one remains stationery. This type of phenomenon has also been witnessed.

After the exodus of the Jews from Egypt led by Moses, there are numerous descriptions of UFO's which seem to have often accompanied them. Of course, the scribes writing the Bible did not use the kind of terminology that we use. They would refer to clouds and Stars with the properties of high speed movement and flight control, as well as fiery chariots and so on. The following extract from the Book of Exodus, Chapter 13, Verses 21 to 22, is a typical example:

"And the Lord went before them by day in a pillar of cloud, to lead them along the way; and by night in a pillar of fire, to give them light; to go by day and night: He took not away the pillar of cloud by day, nor the pillar of fire by night, from before the people."

This description of pillars of cloud and fire is very close to the cigar-shaped description of a UFO. In fact, the Biblical description of a pillar is preferable to the far less evocative one of a cigar! In the 20th century we have become more mundane in our descriptive terminology. Compare, for example, "wheel in the middle of a wheel," with the rather facile term, "Flying Saucer."

The Prophet Elijah was taken to Heaven in a Space vehicle; his follower Elisha was with him at the time and witnessed this, and II Kings, Chapter 2, Verse 11, reads as follows:

"And it came to pass, as they (Elijah and Elisha) still went on, and talked, that, behold, there appeared a chariot of fire, and horses of fire, and parted them both asunder; and Elijah went up by a whirlwind into heaven."

Obviously the chariot and horses represent a vehicle to the Biblical scribes and the whirlwind suggests an apparent vortex of energy which is often described in UFO sightings.

The prophet Zechariah gave a very precise description of a UFO, in Chapter 5, Verses 1 to 2:

"Then I turned, and lifted up mine eyes, and looked, and behold a flying roll. And he said unto me, What seest thou? And I answered, I see a flying roll; the length thereof is 20 cubits, and the breadth thereof 10 cubits."

A roll, of course, would be a similar shape to the cigar-shaped type of object.

Examples from the Bible of UFO activity is not the main purpose of this book. The only reason for including them at all is to put the contacts of Dr. George King in their correct historical context. However, we cannot leave the Judeo-Christian UFO legacy without referring to possibly the most significant and famous Biblical sighting of them all, namely, the Star of Bethlehem. An excerpt from the Book of Matthew, Chapter 2, Verses 9-11, reads as follows:

"And, lo, the Star, which they saw in the east, went before them, till it came and stood over where the young child was. When they saw the Star, they rejoiced exceedingly with great joy. And when they were come into the house, they saw the young child with Mary, his mother, and fell down, and worshipped him."

It is staggering to think that for centuries it was believed that a Star had led the three wise men to a stable in Bethlehem. If a Star were to come near enough to this Planet, assuming that gravity allowed it to do so in the first place, and then pinpointed a country, never mind a city, never mind a young child in a stable in an inn, there would be a dire, Cosmic catastrophe. All the laws of science prove that Stars cannot possibly do that. No, this was a classic example of a UFO, leading three advanced men to a great Interplanetary Master who had been born on this Planet to perform a specific mission.

Dr. King's contacts revealed this kind of vessel is only used by the great Cosmic Masters and is made visible or invisible in accordance with the wishes of the Masters who control them. These Beings are called the Ancient Ones and They control, in an advisory capacity, all humanoid life in the Solar System, as well as that on some Planets in other parts of the Milky Way.

The Star of Bethlehem was one of these great Vehicles of light, in which certain of the Ancient Ones came near to Earth so that They could carry out complicated metaphysical operations, the result of which was the virgin birth of Jesus.

It is worthy of special note that the Avatar Jesus Christ was a Venusian Who came to Earth in answer to a call for help. He saw the dire need of mankind and made the great sacrifices demanded of a compassionate Master in such an exalted position upon the ladder of evolution.

These Vehicles are also used for "Spiritualizing" this Earth. They can change the rate of vibration of every molecule of matter, whether organic or inorganic, in any area they so desire. Whether it be large or small is of no consequence. The existence of all life upon Earth owes its continuance to this type of Divine Intervention. These Vehicles come mainly from Saturn but some come from Jupiter and Uranus. Uranus is referred to as the Great Mother of the System, while the Sun is the Father of our little Planetary System.

The Master Jesus was not, and never claimed to be the one and only Son of God. Such a belief denies the validity of all other religions and is the kind of dogmatic teaching which will gradually disappear as the Aquarian Age dawns in the new millennium. This does not mean to say that Christianity will disappear— far from it. It is a wonderful, living philosophy introduced by a great Master Who originally came from Venus. His origins are referred to in the Book of Revelations, Chapter 22, Verse 16, as follows: "I am the root and the offspring of David, and the bright and morning Star." The bright and morning Star is, of course, Venus.

Conditioning is a very strange thing. We are used to the idea of Jesus being the one and only Son of God. No matter what our own religion may be or where we were born, we know that this is a view held by millions of people around the world, and one which has been held for hundreds of years. Therefore, it seems very familiar. But just for a moment take a detached view, free of conditioning, and look at two possible concepts. One is that God chose to have a Son born in a physical body, in one part of the world, and live for 33 years until He was killed by the Romans. In the whole of our history, God has only seen fit to do this once, thereby providing the one and only way to Truth. Those many people born in other parts of the world, some before His incarnation on Earth, and who therefore will never in their lifetime receive this Truth, are automatically denied the opportunity of the only true religion. That is one view.

Another view is that Interplanetary Beings have been born on this Earth at certain times in our history to bring about Spiritual change in many ways. Jesus was one of these great Cosmic Masters Who, with the help of a Spacecraft that we refer to as the Star of Bethlehem, was born onto this world 2000 years ago, in order to teach the message of Love. He died to manipulate Karma, not to forgive us our sins, which is Karmically impossible, but to bear Karma for the world as a whole. These two concepts are both points of view, but an impartial observer looking at them both would have to admit that, of the two, the idea that He came from another world, and was not the only one to do so, is far less radical from a theological point of view than the idea that He was the one and only Son of God in our entire history.

This is not said to decry anyone's religious beliefs, but to illustrate a point regarding conditioning. If you told an anthropologist, who had never heard of Christianity, that a certain tribe practise an ancient rite in which they drink wine which is symbolic of the blood of God, and eat bread which is symbolic of the body of God, he would label this as a primitive culture with the possibility of cannibalistic tendencies. So let none of us be judgmental in examining beliefs which may appear strange only because they are unfamiliar to us.

THE VEDAS

When you look at other religious scripts you find a very similar pattern of UFO involvement in the Spiritual revelations of our history. The Hindu texts known as the Vedas are a good example of this. As with the Holy Bible, there is no guarantee of the complete accuracy of these writings which, in some cases, were passed down for thousands of years orally before being written down at all. There is therefore a definite margin for error and the chronology may have been incorrectly altered along the way.

Texts like the Ramayana use the Sanskrit word, vimana, which means "flying celestial vehicle." The following is an extract from the Ramayana which is typical of the descriptions of vimanas:

"When morning dawned, Rama, taking the vimana Puspaka had sent him by Vivpishand, stood ready to depart. Self-propelled was that car. It was large and finely painted."

In another extract, a vimana is described as follows:

"That aerial and excellent vimana, going everywhere at will, is ready for thee. That vimana, resembling a bright cloud in the sky, is in the city of Lanka."

It is interesting to note here the reference to "at will" which suggests a stupendous science involving thought control by the occupants, exactly as Dr. King has been informed in his contacts. The Vedas, and indeed the Buddhist scripts, have a concept of life throughout the planetary realms. They fully accept the existence of life on other worlds and life on higher spheres as being part of the same belief in universal consciousness.

One Vedic script describes the liberation of a Maharajah (King) named Dhruva from material bondage into high Spiritual consciousness. This is often referred to in metaphysical writings as the state of Ascension. This amazing experience, which takes on a Cosmic dimension, is described in the Bhagavata Purana, Book 4, Chapter 12, as follows:

"As soon as the symptoms of his liberation were manifest, he saw a very beautiful vimana coming down from the sky, as if the brilliant full moon were coming down, illuminating all the ten directions..."

He was then picked up by this vimana, or UFO, and the following is a description of his journey:

"While Dhruva Maharajah was passing through Space, he gradually saw all the Planets of the Solar System, and on the path he saw all the demi-gods in their vimanas showering flowers upon him like rain...

"Beyond that region, he achieved the transcendental situation of permanent life in the Planet where Lord Vishnu lives."

Not only does this description detail a truly beautiful close encounter of the third kind which took place thousands of years ago, it also indicates that it is possible to attain such a high and elevated state of consciousness, that one is liberated from the need to reside on Earth and can go to other worlds for continued existence. This belief is fundamental to The Aetherius Society, and this example illustrates that such views are not completely new, but have been around for thousands of years before even the Lord Buddha, the Master Jesus or Socrates were heard of. Indeed, scholars do not know exactly how old the Vedic scripts are.

WHY DR. GEORGE KING?

Just one or two examples from both eastern and western religious records have been selected to put into context the extraordinary experiences of Dr. George King. It is absurd to study these wonderful records and then ignore the fact that such things could be happening in our lifetimes. It is only conditioning that makes people think that all the great Spiritual and Cosmic events must have occurred in some dim and distant time in the past. If you have ever held that view then this is an opportunity to put the record straight by bringing you up to date with happenings which are even more significant than these few examples from history, namely, the contacts of Dr. George King.

One of the questions The Aetherius Society is often asked is

Dr. George King in Siddhasana, 1955

why advanced extraterrestrials should pick this one man, Dr. George King, as their sole channel? In answering this, it is first necessary to correct the question. We have never claimed that Dr. King is the sole channel for Beings from other worlds. What we do claim is that he is Primary Terrestrial Mental Channel. In other words, he is the most important channel for communications from other worlds in these days. It would be illogical to give an important communication to one person here, another person there, and so on, when they could use a single source to put their main messages and instructions through for the world as a whole and thereby avoid confusion.

There have, of course, been other people in the lifetime of Dr. King who have had close encounters of various kinds with UFO's and their inhabitants. There have also been many secret communications with advanced Masters in Retreats which were not intended to be revealed to the world as a whole. But he does stand, in this period of history, as an unparalleled source of extraterrestrial contacts.

Independent research shows that there is no other well known claimant who has been in consistent contact with Intelligences from other worlds for over 40 years. There is certainly no one else we know of who has built up a worldwide organization which, for 40 years, has propagated interplanetary communications and cooperated directly with those who gave them in such a potent manner. There has been no extended break in the Mission of Dr. King; no period of years, months or even weeks, when he has taken a sabbatical or a rest from his position as Primary Terrestrial Mental Channel. And, in all this time, during which he has received thousands of communications, there has been no case of contradiction or conflict between the communications delivered by Interplanetary Beings. These facts, even his critics and disbelievers admit, make him completely unique.

He was not chosen for this task because Interplanetary

Beings particularly favoured or liked him, but because he was in the right position to receive these communications. For one thing, he had the necessary abilities to do so. In all the hundreds of lectures and broadcasts he has given around the world about UFO's and related topics, Richard Lawrence has often issued a challenge which, to this date, has never been met. The challenge is to name another person in the west, other than Dr. King, who even claims to have devoted themselves for ten years to the practice of advanced Yoga systems for eight to ten hours a day, as well as doing a job. Dr. King did just that, starting in 1945 after the Second World War. During the war he had served as a section leader in the Fire Service where he and his fellow fire workers played a vital and dangerous role during the Blitz. As soon as the war finished, at the age of 26, Dr. King devoted himself to advanced Yoga practice.

Many stories have been written in the press about this period of Dr. King's life. They generally choose to highlight the fact that, at certain times during this period, he drove a taxi cab, as if something like this could never happen to a taxi driver. Indeed he did drive taxis during this period, as well as other jobs, including running a chauffeur car hire company and working in an oil company. Dr. King is very happy to acknowledge any or all of these professions, but what is so absurd about these press reports is that they highlight a profession which was taken to earn money to live, and not the Yoga training which qualified him for his life's Mission as Primary Terrestrial Mental Channel. It would be just as absurd to entitle the Gospels, which feature the life of the Master Jesus: "God's Son is born as a carpenter"; or the Bhagavad Gita, which features the Teachings of Shri Krishna: "Cowherd teaches liberation from materialism"!

The important thing about the 10 years between the war and his first contact with a Master from another world was that he devoted himself, on top of his jobs, to the practice of Raja, Gnani, Kundalini, Mantra and other forms of the ancient science of Yoga which lead inevitably, if practised diligently enough, to higher states of consciousness. By the time he was first contacted by a Cosmic Master on May 8th, 1954, during an event now known as "The Command," he was already a Master of Yoga. He had gone beyond psychic development and was capable of raising his consciousness to a very high level, which made it possible for Interplanetary Beings to communicate with him telepathically. Just as the people who had close encounters in the Holy Bible and the Vedic scripts were generally people of noted Spiritual calibre—prophets, sages and Masters—Dr. King was chosen because of his level of Spiritual attainment. He could enter Samadhi, the highest state of meditation known on Earth, in which he received hundreds of communications from the Cosmic Masters.

The scene was set for "The Command" by a massive spate of reported UFO sightings following the war. This was partly because of a far greater awareness of Space travel, and partly because of much more sophisticated ways of viewing the skies. There were, in fact, many sightings during the war from both allied and axis pilots who reported seeing strange metal-like objects which they called "foo-fighters." These performed controlled flight patterns around their planes and were never satisfactorily explained by officialdom. They were, in fact, UFO's. In 1946, just after the war, there were many sightings in Europe, especially Scandinavia, where there were mass sightings of silent "ghost rockets," which were never satisfactorily explained either. In the 1950's there were numerous reports of UFO sightings by people from all walks of life. Specifically, there were waves of sightings over France and Italy in 1954. It was into this climate that the first contact by an Interplanetary Master with Dr. King took place.

THE COMMAND

The following is a description, in his own words, of this extraordinary event, known as "The Command," which was to shape Dr. King's Mission and thereby change the world.

"It was about 11:00 am. on a Saturday morning, early in 1954. As is my usual practice on a Saturday morning, I was busily engaged in household chores. Not that you could call my present domicile a house—for if you wanted to swing a cat around within the yellow papered walls, then it would have to be a manx cat, and a little 'un at that. I was performing a tricky feat at that time, trying to dry four plates by shuffling them about rather in the same way that one shuffles a pack of cards. May I warn any 'independent-bachelor-and-proud-of-it-laddie,' that such a procedure—when you come to consider the frequent breakages—costs almost as much as a wife. And this, chaps, without the other amenities which are part of matrimonial union. If it is any consolation, however, I will say that sweeping up the pieces of broken china can be a very good exercise.

"My window was open, and the pale sunshine streamed through. The noise from the busy street below, blended with the tinkling of the plate against plate in such a way as to form a symphony of materialistic activity. The type of activity, the type of noises you could hear in any town or city on the globe on a Saturday morning.

"It all stopped. It stopped with the startling suddenness of a pistol shot.

"'Prepare yourself. You are to become the Voice of Interplanetary Parliament.'

"This was the alien sound which struck my ear drums with a somewhat gentle firmness. The ensuing silence was broken only by the shattering of plates as they slipped from my useless fingers to the floor. I cannot describe the tonal qualities of the voice which uttered this Command. It came from outside of myself—from the empty space of that tiny room—into my mind with a numbing suddenness which made me grasp a chair for support.

"I may have sat there for one, or two hours—I do not know. The room did not seem to exist during that period—neither did time itself. My world of awareness revolved upon a central axis and that axis was a vital, living, vivid memory of the Command which had been given and the way it had come.

"*Prepare yourself! You are to become the Voice of Interplanetary Parliament'*...... Just that, nothing else! No explanation—which I needed, for I had never heard of Interplanetary Parliament.

"Dear readers, I will never forget the week of hopeless frustration which followed. I could not confide in any but a selected handful of acquaintances—none of whom could offer an enlightened explanation. I had not read any books before that time about Flying Saucers, and knew nothing about them save the trifling information which was sandwiched between the sickly layer of sarcasm in the popular press. I would return to that room at night, and almost weep in my terrible loneliness. Something had been there—something which had spoken to me one sentence and departed, leaving turmoil and bewilderment in its wake.

"It is a well-established metaphysical fact—that the Initiate must experience terrible loneliness just before a great event occurs. Though, to a chap like myself, this knowledge did not bring much comfort. I am one of those somewhat unique individuals, who fortunately are not afraid of what they cannot understand. The more difficult the solution appears to be, the more I yearn to work on the problem. Especially does this apply to the metaphysical problems occurring in the higher vibratory frameworks.

"It is a strange thing that most of us leave the obvious till we have tried all the lesser channels. It was eight days after this event, when I decided to listen to the most eloquent voice of all—the educating voice of Silence.

"After very careful practice of 'Pranayama'—a system of Yogic breathing control—I settled down with a firm determination to stay there until some further explanation was forthcoming. I did not have to wait long. For the second time, during that short period, I was shaken to the core by an amazing happening.

"A man walked THROUGH my locked door, across the creaking boards beneath the faded grey carpet, and sat down opposite to me! The battered old chair creaked as it supported his weight! He was dressed in spotless white robes, which seemed to gleam in the green meditative light I was using. But they were real enough. I had heard the faint swish they made as he crossed the room. I recognized my visitor immediately as a modern leader of Spiritual thought in India. He is very much alive at the moment—living in a somewhat rotund physical body in the Himalayas.

"I am not permitted to give the name of the Saint, but I feel sure those of you who study the all-embracing philosophy of the east, will have guessed it easily. After all, the world is one unit of experience, and a study of a part of its philosophy is incomplete. It takes two halves to make a whole.

"My Yogi visitor smiled and I was submerged in a sea of peace which cleansed the wounds of frustration.

"'It is not for you to judge whether you are worthy to be chosen, my son!'

"Oh, my dear friends, and those of you who have read this narrative of my unique experience so far, I trust are included in the category of my friends—how can I explain the joy in my simple heart at that moment? My mind was stripped naked and read and understood by this ... Saint! My unworthiness for what was obviously a great task, had troubled me all the week. But there were greater Beings than I Who had pronounced judgment upon this. It was as though I was a living pawn positioned upon the checker board of life, and some master chessman had gained my consent before making his move. Submerged as I was in that still, deep lake of peace, my soul signified consent to the move. A move, which—in those days—was hidden by the opaque curtain of my simple ignorance. Despite myself, or because of my real self, tears of joy and gratitude trickled down my cheeks.

"His voice was gentle, but held a peculiar penetrating property, as he continued:

"'**The real necessities of the Age—brought about by the unfeeling march of science into the realms of the atom, and the wrong thought and action of the masses—can be met only by those few who are ready to tune in to those emanations now being sent to this Earth, and become the servants of the Cosmic Masters. You are one of the many called upon to prepare yourself for the coming conflict between the materialistic scientist—who has arrived at his conclusions by the cold application of mathematics and the occult 'scientist,' who has arrived at his conclusions through the recognition that God is All. Pray, be still, meditate, and open the door of your heart and mind to the precious waters of Truth.'**

"After delivering this wonderful message, my Yogi visitor gave me detailed instructions in certain practices. He also told me that those people best equipped to help me would be brought into my orbit.

"The Swami, having imparted this information, bowed with the politeness of a race which enjoyed an advanced culture when ancient Britons still painted themselves with woad. Then he made his exit by walking straight through my locked door! I jerked it open immediately, but the long corridor beyond was deserted. My Initiator from the Himalayas had departed into invisibility.

"The rest, some of you know. A group was formed and Yoga was practised very diligently—until I was able to lift my mind into a higher framework of vibration, and in order to tune into the mental relay being radiated by the great Master Aetherius.

"I know now that "The Command" was given by Aetherius Himself, in such a way as to leave no lingering doubts in my mind as to its authenticity. Also, I know that my visitor from the east—coming as he did with instructions soon afterwards must have been in communication with Venus. It must be very clear to all my readers that Flying Saucer research is really an investigation into the real unchangeable Cosmic Laws which constitute the Absolute Itself. And further, I know that the researcher who divorces himself from what may be termed the Spiritual approach, may never learn the important facts concerning our visitors from other Planets."

The Master Aetherius is a very advanced Master from Venus, whose pseudonym "Aetherius" literally means "one who travels through the ethers of Space." It was a name derived from ancient Greek. Subsequent research showed that in the 8th century B.C., the Greek poet, Hesiod, included in a list of celestial Gods one by the name of "Aether." Ether is the mystical element within which all matter exists. Contrary to orthodox belief, there are not four elements, but five—earth, fire, water, air and ether. Ether has mystical properties in that it contains different levels of matter, which are not limited to the purely physical realm of existence. The concept of life on higher planes, as well as higher Planets, is fundamental to The Aetherius Society, which was named after the Master who made this first historic contact.

PRIMARY TERRESTRIAL MENTAL CHANNEL
Everything you are going to read in this book depends upon your acceptance of Dr. King as a genuine contactee with people from other worlds. We do not expect you to believe this just because it is written here. The Aetherius Society is not a "converting" organization. We are not out to convince people that we have a one and only way, because no such thing exists. We certainly do not use persuasive methods to recruit anyone. Sadly, the media tends to characterize any new organization that puts out beliefs which appear to be New Age as some kind of a cult. According to the current usage of the word, The Aetherius Society is not a cult. There are some reprehensible organizations who have debased people's concept of a religious movement and understandably caused mistrust towards anything new. Having said that, it is worth remembering that Christianity was regarded by the Romans as a bizarre and dangerous religious cult. Indeed, virtually all religious movements were regarded as cults when they first started. The Aetherius Society is an extremely open organization, with a leader who has set an exemplary pattern, living very modestly and sticking, in a completely dedicated manner, to what he knows to be true, namely, his contacts with Masters from other worlds.

He was born on January 23rd, 1919, and was psychic as a child. He was born in an agricultural community and his training was in dairy farming. Following the war and his ten years of intensive Yoga practice culminating in "The Command," he founded The Aetherius Society in 1955 in London, England. In 1959 he went to the United States of America, and settled there in the early 1960's. The Society was incorporated as a non-profit religious, scientific and educational corporation on November 22nd, 1960. It has flourished all over the world, publishing numerous books, tapes and CDs by Dr. King and, above all, performing Missions in cooperation with the Cosmic Masters for the salvation and enlightenment of the world.

Dr. King was born under the sign of Aquarius—fittingly, since one of his tasks has been to pave the way for the Aquarian Age. To assess his true merit and thereby discover exactly why he was chosen for this unique task, you need to examine his life's works in detail. In doing so, you can do no better than to follow the advice given at the beginning of this chapter: "Judge a man by results." That statement, made by an advanced Martian communicator, Mars Sector 6, in 1956, continued in the following way:

"Judge a man by his detachment.

"Judge a man by his love for all.

"Judge a man by his acceptance and knowledge of Oneness.

"Judge a man by his wisdom.

"Judge a man by his Cosmic logic.

"Judge a man by his sacrifice—not for himself, not for his wife, not for his family—but for the whole world, YOUR world."

"These are the ways to judge. Judge well, ye men of Terra, and when ye find one who passes the test of your judgment, then follow such a one even to your death."

CHAPTER THREE

The True History of Mankind

*"It was not meant by the real Controllers of the
initial life manifestation upon Terra that
terrestrial man should have sunk so low."*

— *Mars Sector 6*

CHALLENGING ORTHODOXY

The history of mankind is shrouded in mystery.
Archaeologists, evolutionists and anthropologists have pooled
their findings and together have formed theories about his origins. An orthodox view has grown up based on these findings
about the different stages of mankind's development and the
process of evolution which has taken place. But these are only
theories based upon deduction and speculation arising from
specific findings.

From time to time, new facts emerge and some of these
orthodox beliefs are challenged and revised. Although very few
people question the great contribution made by Charles Darwin
to the understanding of our evolution, his views are not regarded as some unalterable holy grail by all modern thinkers. For a
start, the question of the so-called "missing link" has never
been resolved and, to date, no undisputed evidence has been
produced that there really is such a thing. In all the findings of
prehistoric remains, no one has yet produced an example,
acceptable to the scientific community as a whole, of a species
which bridges the gap perfectly between the ape and the
human being. This is not surprising when you know the true
history of mankind on Earth.

Miners and excavators have, from time to time, found extraordinary artifacts which contradict orthodox, archaeological and Darwinian theories. For example, quarriers working near the River Tweed in Scotland in 1844, discovered a length of gold thread in rock eight feet below the ground which was believed to be millions of years old. In 1851, a resident of Springfield, Massachusetts, dropped a piece of auriferous quartz, believed to be a million years old, which broke and revealed a cut iron nail. Even more startlingly, in the same year in Dorset, Massachusetts, a bell-shaped metal object, looking like a chalice or candle holder and inlaid with silver floral patterns, was found 14 feet down inside solid rock. In 1891, an intricate chain of gold was found inside a lump of coal in Illinois, believed to be millions of years old. In 1927, in Nevada, a fossilized imprint of a leather shoe, complete with hand stitching with fine thread, was found in Triassic limestone, believed to be many millions of years old.

Archaeological findings like these occur from time to time, challenging and confounding the orthodox view of mankind's history on Earth. All these manufactured objects suggest that there were previous civilizations on this Earth, millions of years old, which starkly contrasts with Darwinian ideas and challenges his time scale of human evolution. It does not contrast, however, with information received by Dr. George King from other worlds which points to this Planet having been inhabited for millions of years.

At the same time as Darwin was propounding his theories of evolution, another movement was emerging in 19th century Britain, the Theosophical Society headed by Madame Helena Blavatsky. She ridiculed Darwin's assertion that man is descended from the ape. Based upon her contacts with Members of the Great White Brotherhood (the Spiritual Hierarchy of Earth), Who are Masters living in ageless bodies in secret Retreats around the world, she talked about the existence of previous civilizations on this Planet, a view which was to be supported later by archaeological and geological findings.

Madame Blavatsky was not the first person to talk about previous civilizations. There had been knowledge and speculation about a civilization known as Atlantis thousands of years before this. Aelianus, in his work Varia Historia, reveals that Theopompus (c. 400 B.C.) recorded an interview between the King of Phrygia and Silenus, in which Silenus referred to the existence of a continent beyond the Atlantic, larger than Asia and Europe combined.

In his Timaeus and Critias Dialogues in the 4th century B.C., Plato describes Atlantis according to an account which goes back a considerable time before this. It is a story told to Plato by the aged Critias, his maternal uncle. Critias is said to have received it from the written records of a remote ancestor, Dropides, who in turn received these records from a much revered law giver of the Athenians known as Solon. But the account did not even originate with Solon for he claimed to have heard it from an aged Egyptian priest who was a scribe at Sais, a large city in the Nile Delta. He, in turn, had received it from studying Saitic hieroglyphic texts which recorded a previous golden age and the destruction of Atlantis. The philosopher Proclus, who lived hundreds of years later, from 412 to 485 A.D., wrote a detailed commentary on Plato's dialogue in which he stated that 300 years after Solon's voyage to Egypt, in about 260 B.C., a Greek by the name of Crantor came to Sais and saw there, in the temple of Neith, a column completely covered with hieroglyphics, on which the history of Atlantis was recorded. Scholars translated it for him and he testified that their account fully agreed with Plato's account of Atlantis, which he knew well.

The account describes an advanced and civilized race who lived in harmony and mutual respect, and the following excerpt gives an indication of this:

"They therefore did not lose self-control nor were they blind to what in their sober minds they clearly realized: that all this flourished only because of their common goodwill and morality, and that it would perish if they excessively strove for it and overvalued it, and both goodwill and character would be destroyed. Because of this mentality and the continued power of the divine nature, the good fortune we have previously described flourished among them."

Plato goes on to describe that the great culture of Atlantis started to decline when evil entered in, selfishness and greed became paramount, and they were no longer willing to live together in harmony, respecting each other's rights. He continues:

"But, as the godlike strain was gradually diluted among them, because it often was mixed with mortal stock, and human nature gained the upper hand, they became evil, unable to bear their riches with restraint."

As a result of this loss of goodwill, or as Plato describes it, "the continued power of the divine nature," there was a violent end to this civilized culture in the following way:

"But later, when there came violent earthquakes and floods, the entire valiant generation of your people were swallowed up by the Earth, and the island of Atlantis was similarly swallowed up by the sea, vanishing in a single dreadful day and in a single dreadful night..."

Does this remind you of a catastrophe which has been described elsewhere, namely, the Old Testament account of

Noah's Flood? There are embellishments to the Biblical story, such as the idea of animals going into an Ark two by two, which may have been a way for primitive people to understand how the animal population could continue. Despite this, scholars do generally accept most of the Old Testament as an historical account of events. They are continually updating, revising and disagreeing with one another about its chronology and other details, but it is an unique record of some accepted events, mixed in with myth and symbology. The account of the Flood is an accurate description of an horrific event which took place in mankind's history. It is confirmed by other accounts, which have come to light from native cultures in other parts of the world, which talk of massive destruction and flooding in our distant history. The peoples of the Andean region in South America, for example, share different versions of the same basic story. These, too, record a terrifying period when the Earth was inundated by a great flood, and plunged into darkness by the disappearance of the Sun.

NUCLEAR HOLOCAUSTS

The Hindu writings are more specific, indicating that a former advanced civilization used foul weapons of war to bring about this destruction. Hindu texts refer to the "Brahma weapon" or the so-called "weapon of God" (a distorted name, if ever there was one), which was an atomic weapon. Another device referred to in the Hindu scripts was the "Agneya weapon," and the following is a description taken from the Mahabharata which describes its devastating effect upon an earlier civilization:

"A blazing missile possessed of the radiance of smokeless fire was discharged. A thick gloom suddenly encompassed the hosts. All points of the compass were suddenly enveloped in darkness. Evil

bearing winds began to blow. Clouds reared into the higher air, showering blood. The very elements seemed confused. The Sun appeared to spin round. The world, scorched by the heat of that weapon, seemed to be in a fever. Elephants, scorched by the energy of that weapon, ran in terror, seeking protection from its terrible force. The very water being heated, the creatures who live in the water seemed to burn..."

Is this not reminiscent of the ghastly accounts of Nagasaki and Hiroshima?

There are similar echoes of nuclear fall-out in the Biblical story of Sodom and Gomorrah. In the light of the existence of such weaponry, it becomes less a symbolic fable and more an historical possibility. Genesis, Chapter 19, Verses 24-28, read as follows:

"Then the Lord rained upon Sodom and upon Gomorrah brimstone and fire from the Lord out of Heaven; and He overthrew those cities, and all the plain, and all the inhabitants of the cities, and that which grew upon the ground. But his wife looked back from behind him, and she became a pillar of salt. And Abraham got up early in the morning to the place where he stood before the Lord: and he looked toward Sodom and Gomorrah, and toward all the land of the plain and beheld, and, lo, the smoke of the country went up as the smoke of a furnace."

Just as the Greeks had seen the horrific destruction of Atlantis as an act of retribution by Zeus, so the scribe who wrote the story of Sodom and Gomorrah saw it as retribution by the Lord. In fact, these were acts of self-destruction through the misuse of atomic power in the past as we have seen happen again in modern times.

Similar evidence of cataclysmic events in our distant history is deduced from geophysical and geological surveys. It is agreed that terrible, destructive forces must have been unleashed on this Earth many thousands of years ago. By studying the specific nature of the climatic, seismic and geological events linked to the various advances and retreats of the ice sheets around the globe, scientists believe that tidal waves, earthquakes, gigantic wind storms and the sudden onset of glacial conditions took place thousands of years ago. Darwin himself concluded that this turmoil must have shaken "the entire framework of the globe."

As with all scientific studies, it is impossible to be absolutely certain of their accuracy. So many supposed scientific certainties have proved, at a future time, in the light of further findings, to have been primitive miscalculations. However, no matter how much one argues about the details, and particularly the timing, there is no doubt at all that many thousands of years ago, an act of violent destruction took place upon this Planet which had all the hallmarks of nuclear destruction.

It is, therefore, extremely valuable to learn from those Interplanetary Beings Who have watched the progress of our world for millions of years, exactly what did happen. Dr. George King, as Primary Terrestrial Mental Channel, was in a position to do this, and can confirm and expand on the ideas propounded by Madame Blavatsky and the Theosophists. Madame Blavatsky revealed the fact that there were two previous civilizations to our own, known as Lemuria (sometimes called Mu), and Atlantis. She divided mankind's history into seven phases of human existence known as "root races." She regarded Lemuria as the third root race, Atlantis as the fourth, and our current civilization as the fifth. Whether the Atlantis she referred to was the same civilization as that described by

Plato is debatable. It could be that Plato was describing a remnant of Atlantis. Certainly, if it was the same civilization, it existed hundreds of thousands of years earlier than most scholars believe. Cosmic Intelligences date Lemuria as existing millions of years ago and Atlantis as existing at least hundreds of thousands of years ago.

The Cosmic Transmissions delivered through Dr. George King have gone further than any other writings on Earth to explain the true history of mankind. Behind all the activities of Lemuria, which was destroyed in an atomic war, Atlantis, which was also destroyed in an atomic war, and our current civilization, there have been the watchful eyes of great Cosmic Beings, who have not been allowed to directly intervene to prevent us from our nuclear folly, but have helped wherever they were allowed by Karmic Law.

COSMIC HELP

One thing you start to realize when you study Intelligences from other worlds, is that they are indeed alien to our way of thinking. It is no good expecting them to behave in the way that we think we would behave in their position. For example, many people come up with the proposition that if there were intelligent beings on other worlds who were monitoring our civilization here, they would definitely land openly and prove themselves beyond any doubt. They would land in Hyde Park, London; Central Park, New York; or some other prominent, public landmark, and show themselves to everyone. People who make this proposition go on to say that because they do not behave in this way, then they obviously do not exist. Such people are completely missing the point. It is not a question of what we think they would do, it is a question of what the records tell us that they actually have done and continue to do.

They are an extremely subtle, wise people, who know exactly what reaction their activities will have. They know that there will be hostility and resentment from some when they land; they know that others will look to them to solve all our problems without any effort on our own part; and they know that others will continue apathetically and ignore their presence on Earth as long as they possibly can. They also know that there are a few who would respond wholeheartedly to such a landing and cooperate with them. As this number grows, so will the day of their open landing come closer. They will land when enough people are ready to cooperate with them. They cooperate absolutely with the Divine Law, which governs all Creation. They are simply not allowed by this Law to intervene beyond a certain point; to demonstrate their powers and even their existence to unwilling disbelievers beyond a certain point. It is quite extraordinary that, despite the fact that literally hundreds of thousands of people have seen UFO's, the world as a whole does not make a concerted effort to find out what they are and, more importantly, who is manning them. But it does not. It is left to individuals to make their own investigations and come to their own conclusions, as you are doing by reading this book.

In recent years, considerable evidence has been found which points to the fact that Cosmic Beings have helped us at certain times in our history. For example, since the 16th century, several maps have been found in Europe which show the Antarctic region as it was before it was covered by the ice cap. Until the seismic analysis of this region in 1949 by the British/Swedish Antarctic expedition, nobody knew what the region of Antarctica was like beneath the ice cap. Some geologists estimate that this ice cap moved there as a result of a shift of the Earth's crust thousands of years B.C. So how did the European cartographers who drew up these maps over 400 years ago know this information?

One 18th century French geographer, Philippe Buache, seems to depict an even earlier period when there was no ice in the region at all. This reveals sub-glacial topography of the entire continent of Antarctica which was not confirmed until 1958, the International Geophysical Year, when a comprehensive seismic survey was carried out. Some say that millions of years have elapsed in this region since it was completely free of ice. Others say that it was ice-free 15,000 years ago. Either way, how did these cartographers know this topography?

Even more startling than these examples is the existence of a Chinese map, copied from an earlier original onto a stone pillar in 1137 A.D. This accurate map, which uses high quality information about longitudes, was drawn up with the benefit of spherical trigonometry and shares many features of European and Middle-Eastern maps. Not only does this suggest that the Chinese had aerial information about the globe, but that Europe, China and the Middle-East were getting their information from a common source. Whoever mapped this globe had advanced instrumentation which did not exist until comparatively recently. Is not this an indication of help from higher Cosmic Beings?

Another classic example is the Pyramids of Giza. The usual historical explanation of thousands of slaves building these pyramids is becoming increasingly questioned as more and more information comes to light. This is not only because of the superb craftsmanship involved in the construction of these pyramids and the question of transporting the massive stones involved. Archaeo-astronomers, making use of the latest Starmapping computer programs, have now demonstrated that the three world-famous pyramids on Egypt's Giza plateau formed an exact terrestrial diagram of the three belt Stars in the constellation of Orion. How could they have known this information without help from above? These extraordinary findings have been added to in recent years by discoveries in South America where Incas and Mayan tribes people left amazing monuments from their advanced civilizations. Chroniclers from the colonial period in the 16th century who came upon

Inca remains in the Andes area, were staggered at what appeared to be, in the words of one chronicler: "As though some magic had presided over its construction." South American legends speak of giants who had lived there before and advanced beings of great light who had come to help them.

One of the most extraordinary examples is in the city of Teotihuacan, 50 kilometers north-east of Mexico City. Just as at Giza, three pyramids are sited there, not symmetrically, as one might have expected, but with two structures in direct alignment with each other, while the third appears to have been deliberately offset to one side. Analysts have found the correlation between the layout of Giza and Teotihuacan so extraordinary as to be beyond coincidence. In the 1960's and 1970's a comprehensive mathematical survey of these structures was carried out by an American engineer, Hugh Harleston, and presented in 1974 at the International Congress of Americanists. The complex mathematical arrangement among the principal structures of ruins in that area was remarkable. According to Harleston's findings, the relationships between buildings indicated the correct orbital distances of the inner Planets, the asteroid belt, Jupiter, Saturn, Uranus, Neptune and Pluto. When you consider that Uranus was unknown to western astronomers until 1787, Neptune until 1846, and Pluto until 1930, these findings suggest an observational astronomy passed down from former advanced civilizations, or by Cosmic Beings, or both.

One can go on and on quoting such findings—indeed many lengthy tomes have been written about them. But the unique contribution by Dr. King's contacts is that we no longer need to rely on speculation based upon legends, geological and archeological findings and biological remains. We now have the advantage of direct communications with people from other worlds who really know exactly what the history of mankind is. It did not begin with Atlantis or even Lemuria. It did not even begin on this Planet. It began on another Planet, called Maldek, which is now the asteroid belt.

When Dr. King first made the statement that the asteroid belt was at one time a Planet which was destroyed by a nuclear explosion, it seemed sensational. Some years later, astronomers began to speculate on the possibility of the asteroid belt having been a destroyed former Planet orbiting between Mars and Jupiter. Dr. King went further than this. He said that the Planet Maldek, and the Earth civilizations of Lemuria and Atlantis, were all destroyed by atomic bombs and that the same race of people inhabited them all—the human race.

American scientist Doctor Tom Van Flandern, author of *Dark Matter, Missing Planets and New Comets,* disagrees with the current theory that the asteroid belt between Mars and Jupiter is debris left over from the formation of the Solar System. He says a new model shows the more likely possibility is that these asteroids are in fact remnants of a Planet which exploded. It is also postulated by others that it is possible for this Planet to have been inhabited by a hi-tech civilization which developed the technology capable of destroying worlds and perhaps they committed the ultimate horror—destroying their own world.

Professor Ovenden, former astronomer of the Department of Geophysics and Astronomy of the University of British Columbia, Vancouver, went even further. He stated that 25 years of research indicates that the asteroid belt was not only a Planet, but that it exploded approximately 16 million years ago. That figure of 16 million years is not too far from the figure given by the Cosmic Masters through Dr. King of around 18 million years ago, when mankind left the Planet he had destroyed, Maldek, and came to this Earth. Already a civilized race inhabited this Earth, known as Adamic man, who were willing to assist the backward race of people who had destroyed a neighbouring Planet.

Here, in the words of Dr. King, is the full ghastly history of mankind.

MANKIND'S HISTORY

"Millions of years ago there was another Planet in this Solar System. This Planet made an orbit between Mars and Jupiter. It was a small mass about the size of Earth. A green prosperous world inhabited by a people who were, for the most part, reasonably satisfied with their progression. This civilization had not reached a state of really advanced culture, but had nevertheless attained a stage which afforded an abundance of necessities which made life comparatively comfortable for all.

"These people had likes and dislikes, hopes and ambitions, as indeed do you. Male and female caused procreation of the races, as do the people on Earth.

"They studied the philosophies and dabbled in the sciences, as do terrestrials, except that these people were more advanced in many ways than are earthlings. The Planet was so highly mechanized that robots took care of all the menial tasks. The inhabitants had discovered a rudimentary form of Space travel, but soon found that their craft did not possess sufficient cruising range owing to the fact that their fuel was too heavy to allow them to penetrate far into the System. They could control their weather so that drought and famine became long forgotten. The majority, having an abundance of food, having no menial tasks to perform, soon became content to while away their unrecallable hours in the Sun. They became, in comparison with the higher Planetary cultures, a selfish, lackadaisical people seeking after their own enjoyment, as do the majority of terrestrials.

"Then the disease came.

"It probably started subtly in the minds of those few men of science who shunned the procrastinating majority, in a fervent search for material conquest, thus leaving themselves open to the incurable affliction.

"The mental disease manifested itself as a lust for greater power.

"They found it!

"They exploded a hydrogen bomb and completely destroyed the Planet Maldek and murdered the whole populace in one blinding flash of searing flame.

"Not the hydrogen isotope bomb which only releases one ten thousandth part of its force as does the murder weapon on Earth, but the scientists of Maldek discovered how to convert hydrogen mass into energy in its entirety and thus murdered a whole world. All that is now left of that beautiful green Planet, which at one time teemed with life, gaining its expression through experience, is the asteroid belt. Thousands of pieces of cold rock, spinning through Space, lifeless, devoid of atmosphere, a burned, broken, dead world.

"Although the terrible disease, the lust for power and material conquest, affected only a few, the majority of people were so lackadaisical, so confined to their own petty contentment and ease of life that they allowed this horrible Cosmic crime to be committed. They were all just as responsible for this terrible sin as were the few who actually caused it.

"The millions of life streams who inhabited Maldek were suddenly released on to their different etheric planes. According to the perfect Law of Karma, these life streams had to reincarnate again, under strict limitation, upon another Planet in the Solar System. They could not reincarnate upon Jupiter, because even in those days, the inhabitants had reached such a high state of Spiritual culture that the Planet was used as a reception centre for the Interplanetary Confederation, which actually had its seat upon Saturn. Jupiter, with its massive bulk, approximately 630 times the size of Earth, could well accommodate the thousands of representatives coming from different worlds within and even outside of the Solar System, to the seat of learning

Saturn. They could not be reincarnated upon Uranus or Venus because both these peoples had reached such a high state of culture that the involved intelligences from Maldek would not have learned the lessons essential to their further progress. Mercury was already operating as the major communications centre for the Solar System. Mars was already inhabited by an advanced race who were the engineers and builders in the Solar System.

"The Earth was approached.

"The Cosmic Hierarchy first made an appeal to the Earth as an Intelligence, to see if She would agree to withhold Her evolutionary progress and bear the limitations which would be necessarily imposed upon Her should the people from Maldek be allowed to reincarnate.

"The Earth, being a great Planetary Lord, took merciful compassion upon the killers of Maldek and agreed to their reincarnation upon Her back and thereby agreed to the thousands of years of necessary limitation which would have to be imposed during their reincarnation so that they could gain essential experience.

"The Cosmic Hierarchy then approached the true inhabitants of Earth, a highly cultured race of individuals called—Adamic man. Adamic man agreed that he would give place to the reincarnating life streams and he cooperated in such a manner as to make this cycle of incarnation complete.

"Gradually those too lazy to stop the shocking Cosmic crime of the destruction of Maldek and those who had actually brought it about, were reincarnated upon Earth. Adamic man stayed for a time giving instruction, guidance and help to the mutants which plagued the grass of Earth. Then, eventually, when Adamic man had caused some semblance of civilization to be brought into being on Earth, he, obeying his instructions according to the Law, left the human race to its own devices.

"Out of the gross limitation of atomic mutation, the civilization of Lemuria dragged its weary self. It grew in culture. The Earth became somewhat similar to what Maldek had been. The people began to probe the philosophies and the sciences again. The Earth gave of its abundance and the Lemurian civilization flourished.

"In its hey-day, it was a civilization of much finer culture than we know on Earth today. The Lemurians established a liaison between themselves and the Planets Venus and Mars. The Venusians and Martians, not dictating in any way to the Lemurians, nevertheless taught them many lessons.

"But alas, the disease struck again.

"Lemuria was split into two different camps—the White Magicians and the evil black magicians. The White Magicians, learning many things from the Visitors from other Planets, had advanced greatly in metaphysical sciences. The black magicians probed the atom. Again, for the second time, they unlocked the forces within God's tiny building blocks and destroyed the civilization of Lemuria.

"But this time those people who were ready were actually evacuated prior to the destruction of Lemuria by vehicles from other Planets which landed upon Earth in order to perform this evacuation. In fact, even the evil forces were warned time and time again of their folly, but alas they took no notice and died as a result.

"Again, those left were born through gross limitation on and off a world seething with radioactive poisoning until, eventually, after thousands of years, another semblance of a culture came into being and, slowly at first, then later gaining momentum, the civilization of Atlantis flourished upon Earth. Again Space travel was established. Again some listened to the voice of Wisdom coming from Higher Sources and there was a split into three definite camps. The few, searching for a force to give them conquest over the whole Solar System; the majority not caring much, because they were content to live in their procrastinations; and the other few, who had proved themselves ready for the higher teachings and possessed the logic and faith to accept the voice of Higher Authority. There was a great mental battle on Atlantis between the White Magicians and the evil practitioners of the black arts. Again the sadistic minds of the dark ones unlocked the pandora's box and invented two atomic weapons. They quarrelled among themselves. One side made a weapon called 'Indra's dart,' which was an atomic bomb, and the other side invented a controllable atomic ray called—surprisingly enough, the 'Brahma weapon' or 'weapon of God.'

"Now the Martians, who had been in close liaison with the White Magicians on Atlantis, saw that a great war was brewing between the two evil factions and landed five large Spacecraft upon Earth called, 'Cities of Shan.'

"The White Magicians, and indeed all those who were ready for evacuation just prior to the outbreak of atomic war, were taken off the Earth. The evil forces, beset with greed and lust for material supremacy, warred with each other. As neither side could win such an atomic war—down fell the civilization of Atlantis into charred radioactive ruins.

"It is a strange thing that, if this truth were written as a novel, no one would ever accept it to be in anyway feasible or logical. No thinking man would believe that a race of intelligent people could, three times in succession, make the same mistake, although twice previously they had been forced to suffer gross limitation for this very mistake. No humanitarian would ever believe, were this written as fiction, that people could have been so absurdly foolish as the people upon Earth have been.

"But, believe it or not, this is a brief resume of what is written in the always truthful Akashic records.

"So much for the past—what about today?

"Again the forces of the atom have been unleashed. Again the world is divided against itself. Again we stand in a similar position to the one we occupied before the destruction of Maldek, before the destruction of Lemuria. We stand in a similar position now, as you read this, to the one we stood in before the atomic destruction of Atlantis.

"It should also be noted that, after the destruction of Lemuria, the Cosmic Hierarchy saw fit to place a barrier around the Earth called, in some occult books, 'the ring-pass-not.' In physical terms this barrier is called—the ionosphere. After the destruction of Atlantis, 'the ring-pass-not,' or ionosphere, was greatly intensified. This intensification tended to cut man off from the higher forms of inspiration as a well-deserved limitation, making advancement so much more difficult for him. This move had to be brought about according to Karmic Law. But it should also be appreciated that both in Atlantean and modern times, man has always had access to the philosophies and the definitions of the Divine Laws. In modern times, this access was made possible through the Wisdom propounded by Interplanetary Avatars such as Shri Krishna, Buddha, Patanjali and the Master Jesus, who came to Earth to teach and in the case of the latter, to die to save terrestrials from a catastrophe. Mankind, even in his darkest hour, has never been left alone. He chose to disregard the teachings of the Great Ones, thereby exercising his petty freewill which has led him into the troubles which he has faced.

"This is a very brief history of why man is here upon Earth and why he is at the bottom of the evolutionary ladder in this Solar System. No other peoples in the Solar System have committed the worst possible crime, namely, that of murdering a Planetary Intelligence."

In these days we have reached exactly the same point that Maldek reached and failed, Lemuria reached and failed, and then Atlantis reached and tragically failed again. We have unleashed nuclear power and with it the ability to destroy our world. Governments have behaved irresponsibly with the nuclear arsenals at their disposal. But this time it can be different. The quotation by Mars Sector 6 that this chapter started with reads in full as follows:

"It was not meant by the real Controllers of the initial life manifestation upon Terra that terrestrial man should have sunk so low, should have brought about such a sequence of deterioration, but, alas, this has happened. However, that selfsame man, radiant as a veritable spark and spirit of God Itself, can rise from his present state into a state predetermined by the higher aspects of man itself."

How can we do this? The answer to that question is found in the study and, more importantly, the practice of the Space Message.

CHAPTER FOUR

The Space Message

"A new language will be brought into being.
This is to be the language of—Direct Action."

— *The Master Aetherius*

COSMIC CONTACTS

According to a recent survey of a large number of close encounters, the two most consistent messages that witnesses claim to receive from Interplanetary Beings are: that we are all one people regardless of colour, class or creed; and that we must desist from atomic experimentation which is extremely dangerous, not only to our world but to the Universe as a whole.

In examining the claims of close encounters with extraterrestrial intelligences, you need to use a lot of discrimination. There have been a considerable number of hoaxers and probably even more deluded people who claim to have been in contact with people from other worlds. There are, however, some genuine contactees of which the most significant in this century is Dr. George King. Some researchers ignore Dr. King's claims for two main reasons. Firstly, they are religious in nature and many researchers do not wish to go near anything religious. Secondly, they are very authoritative and they answer the questions that many researchers make a living, or a hobby, out of not knowing the answers to. Facts, however, are facts and Dr. King has been in communication for over forty years with people from other worlds. In order to receive Cosmic contacts, Dr. King has used two main methods: a pure form of telepathic communication in which he writes down the messages; and a mediumistic Samadhic trance condition in which the Cosmic

Masters speak through him using his larynx, in which the messages are tape recorded. Of these two, trance has been used for the most important Cosmic Teachings and in 1957, Dr. King gave the following explanation of why he used this condition.

"I have been asked several times why a trance condition is employed in order to receive the mental transmissions radiated by Aetherius and other Interplanetary Communicators.

"Let me start with the consideration of two major aspects of the problem, namely:

"**1.** What is a mental transmission?

"**2.** What type of trance condition is employed?

"**1.** What is a mental transmission?

"A mental transmission, in this case, has certain of the qualities of a normal radio transmission, except that different frequencies are used. The Interplanetary Communicators are able to transmit their thoughts upon a magnetic beam which acts as a carrier wave. This beam or carrier wave can be directed by their applied mental pressures with almost uncanny accuracy towards any human being whether capable of conscious reception or not. The radiation is not limited to distance between transmitter and receiver, neither is it limited by differing vibratory octaves of existence. In other words, Aetherius is capable of transmitting His thought waves in a predetermined pattern over great physical distances and from different planes of existence. For example, He has transmitted from Shamballa, existing in etheric substance, to Earth, existing in material substance. At other times, Mars Sector 6 has transmitted from a physical vehicle describing an orbit around the world, the Third Satellite, to myself in the Caxton Hall, London. In both these cases I was able to cause the resistance required in order to bring about translation into sound of these carefully directed series of thought impulses, even though the transmissions were radiated from different planes of manifestation.

"It should be understood that in order to be a good channel for the reception of these directed thought impulses, the medium should be capable of (a) reception and (b) translation into sound of the stimuli, without any discolouration caused by the pattern of personal opinion which is, in most people, a dominating influence. This is where a trance condition can be used with advantage. Which brings us to the second part of the problem.

"**2.** What type of trance condition is employed?

"There are several types and depths of trance conditions, all of which appear to be the same under purely surface examination. All these types can be classified under two main headings, namely: negative and positive conditions.

"The negative type of trance is generally brought about by negating the thinking process so that the 'sensitive' is open to be 'controlled' by another intelligence. Such a procedure opens out the mental and emotional bodies of the medium to 'control' by any entity who has such a desire. The 'controls' are nearly always discarnate entities—some of them, if one is to judge by results, are less evolved than the medium who adopts this highly dangerous practice. Sometimes the medium himself may have the highest desire to serve his fellowmen, but may lack sufficient knowledge of practical metaphysics to enable him to differentiate between good and bad 'controls.' Leave the negative condition alone for you will learn more through the study of good mystical books than ever you will by this practice, and avoid the unspeakable dangers which lurk in the mire of such an approach.

"The positive trance condition is a very different thing, for this is actually brought about by the medium himself in order to tune in to a specific mental radiation. For the Adept, this is not a hit or miss procedure but an exact mental science, consciously applied, in order to bring about a specific result.

"The Yogic trance condition is employed by me in order to tune into and receive the mental stimuli directed by the Interplanetary Communicators. I have learned how to raise the psychic current (Kundalini) from the lower centres and lodge it in a certain higher chakra in order to activate that centre to such a degree that prolonged concentration upon the actual carrier beam which conveys the thought transmission is possible. At the same time, I completely detach myself from the results of the sound translation to such an extent that my own pet likes, dislikes and opinions of the conscious mind cannot discolour the actual message itself. If I do fall short of this goal in any way, it can be put down to my personal imperfection rather than any fault occurring in the actual mental transmission originally received.

"It is of course possible to receive a series of telepathic impressions while still being fully conscious of one's immediate surroundings. But to share an experience with others at the same time, by translating the whole series into sound or speech needs a positive type of Yogic trance condition. Perhaps the greatest lecture I have ever heard was given to me by Aetherius while I was travelling on top of a bus! And this stream of illumination lasted for two whole hours. During the time I was detached from, yet dimly aware of, my immediate environment. I was not in a deep trance condition. Yet I could not have spoken out the words of the Master for the whole period without employing a deep trance condition. Maybe a phrase or two could be spoken but not the whole message exactly as received. Therefore, when condensed, the answer to the problem posed by the original question 'why trance?' is:

"**1.** What is a mental transmission?

"It is a transmission of a specific pattern of thought impulses radiated on a magnetic carrier wave.

"**2.** What type of trance condition is employed?

"A positive Yogic condition, self precipitated by a control imposed upon the currents of psychic energy in order to receive and translate into sound these thought impulses."

DANGERS OF RADIOACTIVITY

It is interesting that the survey of close encounters referred to is consistent with some of the early messages received by Dr. King, messages which probably predated most, if not all, of the claims included in this survey. The essential message of Oneness among all peoples on Earth, and even beyond the Earth, is an integral part of the Space message. They do not regard terrestrial people as coming from different races, cultures, or even countries, but as one unified people.

The early Cosmic Transmissions (communications) received by Dr. King while in Samadhic trance, also concentrated very heavily on the dangers of atomic experimentation, dangers that are still with us today. They warned of the dire effects this would bring and much of this has been verified since. Scientists at New Brunswick University in Canada have established a link between underground nuclear tests and earthquakes. When the French tested a nuclear device in the Pacific in 1988, earthquakes hit North America. The Los Angeles earthquake of 1994 followed a test in Nevada. The terrible earthquake which killed thousands in Armenia happened two days after a Soviet test. And the French Pacific tests in 1995 were followed by volcanic eruptions and earthquake activity. According to these scientists, the energy created builds up underground until it finds a weak spot on the Earth's crust. This is just one example of the change in approach by scientists to nuclear experimentation when compared with their overwhelming confidence in the 1950's.

From the mid 1950's, The Aetherius Society published extraterrestrial warnings about nuclear power. Information about the well-known nuclear accident which took place at Windscale—now Sellafield—on October 10th, 1957, was published by The Aetherius Society in the journal "Cosmic Voice," Issue No. 13, December 1957 to January 1958, in an article entitled "The Windscale Blunder." On October 29th, 1957, a Cosmic Master revealed that our scientists have not even attempted to give us a true picture of the full damage done in this accident by the escape of plutonium dust, radioactive iodine and strontium 90. The then prime minister, Harold Macmillan, stated to the House of Commons on November 8th of that year: "There is no evidence that this accident has done any significant harm to any person, animal or property." Two independent committees of enquiry, consisting of scientists and so-called experts, set up by the Atomic Energy Authority on October 15th, 1957, and the Medical Research Council on October 29th, 1957, produced the so-called evidence on which this statement was made. Since then, British Nuclear Fuels Ltd. has paid out hundreds of thousands of pounds in compensation to the families of cancer victims among the workers of Sellafield. The incidence of leukaemia in people born since this accident, and living in the community of Seascale near Sellafield, is far higher than the national average.

Testing of atomic bombs was considered routine and safe in the 1950's by scientists and political authorities around the world, with very few people speaking out against them. One such person was Dr. George King who conveyed the messages he had received from extraterrestrial communicators, such as the following one from the Master Aetherius:

"When an atom bomb is exploded, you have virtually a three-fold result: 1) heat, 2) radioactive waves, 3) etheric distortion caused by the release of an energy which has hitherto been held in a state of potentiality...

"The whole atmosphere of the Earth is now and always has been radioactive. The whole atmos-

pheric belt of your Earth is filled with minute atomic explosions, but these are under a control which has been predetermined by natural mathematics, so as to afford you with only the rain that you need. It is obvious that any strain upon, or any distortion of the ether, caused by what is to you a little thing —wrong thought—can cause droughts and famines or great floods. So obviously, a tremendous play of etheric disturbances, such as that caused by the release of electro-magneto-motive power, which comes from the bombardment of unstable uranium 238 under high vacuum by slow neutrons, must have great effects upon the weather of your world..."

It is now generally regarded as a fact that major meteorological changes have resulted from atomic releases. The full reasons for this are still being studied by experts, but the one major factor which needs to be understood by science is that radioactivity does not just affect the physical level of existence, but also affects six higher levels in the ethers. The ramifications of this are devastating. For one thing, if you hold the false belief that on dying you pass to some other dimension unrelated to this world, or any other planetary body, you feel less responsibility for the physical world. If, on the other hand, you realize that any etheric distortions that occur here affect other realms of existence, and that they affect your own higher bodies and those of others as well, your sense of responsibility for the here and now is that much greater. A great Cosmic Master from Jupiter, speaking from Satellite 216, said the following:

"We can measure all the octaves of manifestation of this dangerous energy...

"These types of radiation are having a direct effect upon the subtle bodies of all people who pass on from their present existence to the other realms. It would be a fine lesson if all of you atomic scientists could really view your own subtle bodies now. If you could view the astral bodies of the many poor little children who died in Hiroshima and Nagasaki, this would teach you all a great lesson."

Another communicator, Mars Sector 6, speaking about the danger of etheric distortion caused by nuclear experimentation, went as far as this:

"The subtle aspects of radiation brought about as a direct result of chain reaction are very much more dangerous than the more apparent physical manifestations."

In August 1955, the Cosmic Masters, speaking through Dr. King, warned about the genetic effects of radioactive release, the dangers of leukaemia, cellular mutation, cancer of the bone and other parts of the anatomy, and idiocy. All of these facts are now generally recognized by science. They were published in 1961 in the book *You Are Responsible!* and it is a tragedy they were not listened to then. Also published in this book was one of the most outstanding confirmations of the authenticity of Dr. King's communications. In 1978, the highly respected magazine "New Scientist" in Britain, admitted that they had been "scooped by a UFO," regarding the Russian atomic accident in 1958. They had published information from the recently defected Soviet scientist, Dr. Zhores Medvedev, in 1976, concerning this hitherto secret atomic accident in the Urals district of Russia, which had taken place 18 years earlier, and claimed it as a scoop themselves. However, what they did not know at the time was that The Aetherius Society's journal, "Cosmic Voice," Issue No. 16, June/July 1958, had published information from an Interplanetary Intelligence, announcing details of this accident, including approximate figures of those injured and killed, which were very close to the report Dr. Medvedev gave 18 years later. How did Dr. King, who was in Devon at the time, know about this accident which was hidden from the world until 1976? How did he manage to publish this information in his journal, which incidentally, was logged with the British Museum Library in 1958? Only because he had received the information direct from an Interplanetary Intelligence Who had observed this event taking place.

NEW AGE

Certainly the nuclear dangers are one of the main reasons there is an increasing observation of this Earth by people from other worlds. But another vital reason for their great interest at this time, and the series of Teachings they have delivered through Dr. King, is the fact that we are on the verge of a great New Era—the Age of Aquarius is shortly upon us. In the Age of Aquarius we will see a merging of science and religion; a breaking down of the barriers between different religions and cultural and racial groups; the introduction of mysticism into orthodox thinking to bring a deeper realization about the meaning of life in all aspects; and, above all, a much clearer realization and recognition of the importance of Service to humanity.

There was a time when serious Spiritual aspirants of differing religious and cultural backgrounds were taught to pursue their own enlightenment to the exclusion of all else. It was believed that until you were enlightened you were not really in a position to serve and help mankind as a whole effectively enough. Therefore, you should make your first priority your own advancement and then, and only when you are ready, devote yourself in Service to your fellow man. Of course, some of these aspirants made a big mistake by enjoying the process of self-development so much that they forgot the reason they were doing it. They became so preoccupied with their own advancement that they never came out in Service and by doing so, became just as selfish, although more Spiritually developed, as the purely materialistic thinker, who usually has little concern for the welfare of the world as a whole. This was never the intention behind the great Cosmic Plan which brought to Earth such illuminated Teachings as Hinduism, Taoism, Buddhism, various branches of Yoga philosophy, Sufism and Jewish and Christian mysticism. Service has always been the ultimate goal—but in the past it was taught that you had to prepare yourself before you were ready to serve.

The Cosmic Plan has now changed this emphasis. The order of the day now is Service to others, whether you regard yourself as being ready or not. Of course, Spiritual evolution should not be neglected and The Aetherius Society runs numerous courses on various methods of mental, psychic and Spiritual development. But the main emphasis now is Service to the world as a whole. Masters of the calibre of the Lord Buddha, Lao-Tse, Sri Krishna, Sri Patanjali, Sankacharya and others, have visited this Earth from other worlds in order to deliver great paths towards enlightenment. In most cases, these paths have not been followed very actively, and now time has run out. We are living in the nuclear age and even more importantly than that, we are living at a time of change for the Planet upon which we live, the Mother Earth Herself.

This great change has affected the whole evolutionary process of mankind. No longer is it acceptable to concentrate on one's own development to the exclusion of all others. In these days, we are our brother's keepers and whether we are enlightened or not, we must take part in the great plan of Service to others.

KARMA

Crucial to understanding the philosophy of The Aetherius Society is the concept of Karmic manipulation. Many people who talk about Karma do so with a sense of foreboding, as though it is inevitably something negative. It is not. Karma is the great, all-pervasive Law of the Universe—it is an expression of true Divinity. It is completely just and is tempered with compassion. "Whatsoever a man soweth that shall he also reap," says St. Paul in Galatians, Chapter 6, Verse 7; "for every action there is an equal and opposite reaction," says the Buddhist teaching. These are ways of looking at Karma, which is not intended to bring retribution or punishment, or even selfish reward, but to guide us towards a goal of Spiritual realization. Karma guides all life towards this goal, which is ultimately a return to Divinity from where we all came in the beginning. Dr. King has described Karma as pressure, which explains brilliantly how it operates in our lives.

The Cosmic Masters tell us that we can manipulate our Karma. We can take charge of our Karmic patterns by performing Service to others, and this will bring in return greater opportunity, power and enlightenment so that we can do more and more for others and ourselves. In short, by sending out positive energy, we will get positive energy back. Instead of Karma being seen merely as a negative pressure upon us, correcting and teaching us the error of our ways, we can regard it as a great force for good, helping us to advance and progress in all ways.

One of the finest ways to do this is through the giving of Spiritual Healing. The book *You Too Can Heal* by Dr. George King, revolutionized the healing movement in Britain when it was first published in 1976. Until then, healing was looked upon as a gift of the few—you either had it or you did not. With this book came a concept which is now being embraced around the world, that anyone can learn to heal. The Aetherius Society has run healing courses for thousands of people, enabling them to give tens of thousands of healing treatments, both through contact healing (the laying on of hands), and absent healing (over a distance). It is also possible to practise self-healing.

The beauty of Spiritual Healing is that it works in conjunction with other forms of medicine, working on the etheric or auric structure which is interlinked with the physical body. The concept of holistic medicine fits in perfectly with Spiritual Healing, incorporating the whole body and even psychic and mental aspects as well. Most illnesses have, at least partially, a psychosomatic origin. These psychosomatic imbalances can be treated directly by transmitting Spiritual Energy into the aura of the patient. Spiritual Healing is very different from faith healing. It is a scientific procedure of transmitting energies through the psychic centres in the palms of the hands of the healer into the patient. Anyone can do it—including you. By giving healing or any other form of Spiritual Service, you are cooperating directly with the Law of Karma in helping others to overcome their Karmic difficulties. In doing so, you will start to create a positive and more fortunate Karmic pattern in your own life.

LIFE AFTER DEATH

The first obvious question which arises from understanding the Law of Karma is: what exactly happens after death? This question should be properly answered in all the major orthodox religions, but sadly is not. The western idea is that you either go to heaven or hell, depending on your deeds, is based on reincarnation, but sometimes without a logical evolutionary concept. The idea that you would be reborn as an insect, followed by a human, followed by a fish, hardly gives any sense of continuity. So, one needs to turn to metaphysical teaching on this subject.

The Cosmic Masters teach that there are six vibrational frequency levels, or realms, above this physical realm. When your physical body dies, you—that is, your mind and soul which is the real you—goes to one of these realms for a waiting period. The realm you go to will be determined by your deeds in this life and the level of Spiritual realization you have attained. This is not so much a question of punishment and redemption as natural law—you go to the frequency level at which you naturally vibrate. There are also four lower astral realms, which are often termed as "the hells." After a period of waiting on one of these higher or lower realms, you—that is, the soul of you— will choose the time and place of your rebirth. This rebirth will be designed to give you the experiences you need to evolve towards perfection.

There have been many studies made of reincarnation and it is probably the most popularly held religious belief in the world. A Gallup opinion poll in the early 1990's revealed that one in four Americans and Western Europeans believes in reincarnation, mostly as a result of personal experience. Considering that the natural home of this belief has always been the east, many find this a surprising statistic. In another Gallup poll, no less than 65% of respondents had visited a place they felt they had been to before, but had not physically been to in this life.

Perhaps the most telling case for reincarnation, which skeptics really have no satisfactory answer to, are those many incidents of children who are born with extraordinary abilities. One would expect to find children with unusual aptitudes, but not specific technical skills which could only have been learned in a former life. Examples include understanding musical notation without being taught it and being capable of architectural drawing to a high degree of proficiency despite being autistic. Perhaps most convincing of all, there are cases of children who have the ability to speak a foreign language which they have never been taught in this life. In Norway, for example, a set of two-year old triplets proved they could speak a language resembling Finnish, which was not their language of birth. They retained the ability to speak this language until they were four years old.

We live many lives learning the numerous lessons we need in order to gain mastery over experience, which is the purpose of our existence. When you realize that there is no such thing as death, but that we are making a journey of evolution through countless lives, things start to take on a meaning they never had before.

Many of the Cosmic Transmissions received by Dr. King deal with Teachings designed for the New Age. By following these you will enhance your life in all ways and more importantly, help build the New Age. Out of all these Teachings, a series of Transmissions entitled "The Nine Freedoms" ranks as the most complete guide to human evolution ever delivered to Earth.

THE NINE FREEDOMS

No published work goes further to explain this process of evolution, its purpose and fantastic possibilities now and in the future, than *The Nine Freedoms*. This brilliant treatise of true New Age philosophy was delivered by Mars Sector 6 through Dr. George King, between February 12th and March 15th, 1961. It consists of nine texts, each marking a phase in our evolutionary process, and the essential steps we all must take in order to go into enlightenment and beyond. It also includes explanatory commentaries by Dr. King on each Freedom.

Up to this date no work had produced a concept beyond the eastern idea of Nirvana, or the western idea of Heaven. Of the two, Nirvana explains more fully the highest state of existence which can be attained. There comes a stage, according to Eastern religion, when an individual breaks the bonds which tie him to the reincarnatory process on Earth. He enters the most elevated state of consciousness which it is possible to attain, and then becomes free of all attachment, all limitation and merges with the Divine Essence. This is only attained when he has mastered all the necessary lessons on this Planet.

But "The Nine Freedoms" goes beyond this. The role of The Aetherius Society, from a teaching point of view, is not to replace any existing religion but to enhance them all by introducing a Cosmic Concept for the New Age. "The Nine Freedoms" gives a much wider picture than ever before of where mankind is going. The Freedoms are as follows: Bravery, Love, Service, Enlightenment, Cosmic Consciousness, Ascension, Interplanetary Existence, Saturnian Existence and Solar Existence. It is necessary to study the texts and commentaries to fully appreciate what each of these stages means. However, this is a summary of some of the lessons taught in this metaphysical work.

First, it is necessary to break the bonds of conditioning which people from all cultures fall into and this takes bravery. It is quite extraordinary really that people, who choose to follow a religion, unquestioningly accept usually the religion into which they were born as being the one true religion for them. There is no logical reason why they should do this. Why should they believe that their parents were more correct than people living on the other side of the world about religion? It is only because of a conditioned acceptance, that most people follow the religious or philosophical path, usually halfheartedly, into which they were born. It takes bravery to examine Truth wherever you find it and make your judgement accordingly, no matter what effect this may have on those around you.

Love has been very misunderstood. It is generally associated with basic emotional and sexual relations. Most people consider love to belong in the family and only have a small idea of the concept of a universal love for all peoples, and indeed all life, including even so-called inanimate objects. This type of universal, impersonal love is a definite mark of evolution and is something which can, and should, be cultivated.

Service is the most definite mark of evolution. Someone who is serving others, whether or not they are people he or she knows or even likes, is definitely well on the way to Spiritual advancement. Notably, the Freedom of Service comes before Enlightenment. There is an urgency at this time; it is a time of change; it is a time when we should no longer wait for our own advancement, we must get on and serve in Spiritual ways, and this Freedom tells us the many ways of doing so.

Enlightenment is not a state of intellectuality, or even a state of intelligence; it is a state of Being. It is achieved by someone who has mastered mental and psychic development, and gone on to the next essential stage—that of Spiritual mastery over their lower self. This Freedom explains this true state of Enlightenment.

Cosmic Consciousness is a state even beyond Enlightenment. Indeed it is a state beyond mind. It is a state of complete oneness, not just with all life on this Earth, but all life throughout the Universe. Mastery and control of Cosmic Consciousness is the last major step which is necessary on this Earth before freedom from rebirth is attained.

Ascension is this state of freedom from rebirth. It is the ultimate Initiation which is attained by all those who have mastered the basic lessons of life on Earth. Members of the Spiritual Hierarchy of Earth, known as the Great White Brotherhood, have mastered Ascension and have chosen, of their own volition, to stay on Earth in Retreats inside mountains in order to help guarantee the evolution of mankind. Many of these are secret, but some of those that we do know of include: the Himalayas; the Andes Mountains in South America; Grand Teton, Mount Shasta and Castle Peak in North America; Ben MacDhui in Scotland; and Mount Kilimanjaro in Africa. There are also Great White Brotherhood Retreats in other parts of the world.

At this stage "The Nine Freedoms" goes beyond all previous

Teachings, including the great mystical schools of Theosophy, Rosicrucianism and even the Vedas. For the Seventh Freedom is "Interplanetary Existence." At this stage the advanced soul is able to go to another Planet in the Solar System and this Freedom describes the experiences he will enjoy there. These interplanetary races are living on higher frequencies of vibration than those around our Earth, and therefore, they cannot necessarily be seen or detected by Space probes—but they are there. Scientists who tell us there is no life on any other Planet in this Solar System mean by this that we cannot live on any other Planet in this Solar System. They are not aware yet of the etheric life which exists on this world and throughout the Universe at a higher level or frequency of vibration than our own.

Saturnians are the highest and most advanced race in this Solar System. They are revered by all other planetary races, with the sole exception of this Earth. It is not by chance that Saturn is considered by astrologers to represent the influence of the Karmic Law. Saturnians are very Holy Beings and have immense Spiritual power at Their disposal, which They use throughout this Solar System and beyond for the betterment of all life.

There is even life on the Sun, referred to as "Solar Existence." The Lords of the Sun are extremely advanced Beings Who work ceaselessly in radiating Their life-giving energies for the benefit of all life in this Solar System and throughout the Galaxies. We are all virtually solidified sunlight and all energy comes from and through this Sacred Orb, directed by the Lords Who, at a very high frequency of vibration, reside there.

THE TWELVE BLESSINGS

While *The Nine Freedoms* is the major philosophical work of The Aetherius Society, *The Twelve Blessings* is the major religious work. Like "The Nine Freedoms," it is designed to introduce a Cosmic concept for the New Age. It was delivered by the Master Jesus as an extension to the Sermon on the Mount, through Dr. George King in deep Samadhic trance in London between July 27th and October 12th, 1958.

The Twelve Blessings is not just a work for study, it is even more, a practice which is performed regularly by Members and sympathizers of The Aetherius Society all over the world. It can be performed in groups or individually, in any suitable location, whether outdoors or indoors. It consists of Blessings to the following twelve sources:

They Who Work for Peace
The Wise Ones
They Who Love
The Planetary Ones
The Thanksgivers
They Who Heal
The Mother Earth
The Mighty Sun
The Supreme Lords of Karma
The Great Being known as The Galaxy
The Supreme Lords of Creation
The Absolute

The practice of "The Twelve Blessings" is the most beautiful and powerful system of Prayer which can be performed in these days. By doing it, you will help to change the world, as well as alter your own Karmic pattern for the good. You send out Spiritual Energy through the palms of the hands, which are raised, and the psychic centre in the aura known as the heart centre or chakra. It is necessary to use the power of creative visualization to picture white light leaving the palms of the hands and the heart centre, which is a few inches in front of the body, at the central point of the breastbone. After some practice you will start to feel this energy flowing through you. The focus of these Blessings include some of the most significant sources in the Universe. By the Law of Karma, what you send out must be returned to you, so the practitioner receives back from these sources a far higher quality of energy and power which he can then use in his life. This manipulation brings energy from these Cosmic Sources back to this world where it is desperately needed at this time. In the original plan, "The Twelve Blessings" were not due to be delivered at that time, but were delivered at least fifty years early in view of the potential crisis existing on our world in these dangerous days. They are intended to be used as a practice for the New Age. As much as any other practice which can be performed in these days, the performance of "The Twelve Blessings" will manipulate the Karma necessary to bring about the great Spiritual change which is so desperately needed on our world.

The Aetherius Society not only practises Prayer, often combined with eastern Mantras, but also teaches dynamic Prayer in special courses to those who wish to enhance their ability to channel Spiritual Energies, which are the most valuable commodity in our world, way above any precious substance or financial amount. There has been an increased awareness recently of the vital need to perform charity, which is much to be welcomed. The giving of wealth and material help to those in desperate situations is absolutely essential. But to get to the root of the real problems of mankind, the only lasting answer is Spiritual action. This means a direct involvement in the affairs of mankind through the radiation of Spiritual Energy throughout the world. This is what the Master Aetherius was referring to when he announced, in a Cosmic Transmission through Dr. King on November 4th, 1956, the introduction of a new language of Direct Action. This announcement was a result of a meeting of evolved Masters from this world and beyond on the mystic "Island" in the higher realms known as

Shamballa. After making this announcement, which opened this chapter, the Master Aetherius continued:

> *"The decision was made in this way so that all who heard it could meditate upon that sentence, exactly as pronounced.*
> *"I strongly recommend you to do so."*

CHAPTER FIVE

Solving the Energy Crisis

"This Energy is offered to you.
You have but to request it."

— Mars Sector 6

SPIRITUAL ENERGY

Dr. George King has identified the major crisis which is facing us all on this Earth at this time as we prepare for the New Age. He expressed this concept very clearly in a lecture entitled "The Spiritual Energy Crisis," delivered at the American Headquarters of The Aetherius Society in Hollywood in 1973, from which the following extract is taken.

"You have been told, and quite rightly, that the whole of Creation is not only made up of energy, but there is free energy running through it. Mankind can worry about the physical energy crisis which faces him today and will face him tomorrow and in the future, but unless he puts the Spiritual Energy crisis right, he will always be faced with a physical energy crisis. No matter what inventions he comes up with, he will still run short of physical energy—unless he solves the Spiritual Energy crisis; unless he learns how to use what we term Spiritual Energy correctly, and when he does this, then no shortage of physical energy can be allowed to hold up his main journey.

"When you leave home you travel through space and time, but you also make another journey which includes space and time: you make a journey through evolution. The motion through evolution of a point of consciousness is the only real journey. Everything else is a part of this. The journey through space and time is made because of the journey through evolution. Man's limited conception of space and time gives him only a fraction of the picture. To understand space and time you have to understand evolution, and unless you do, you cannot understand the other things.

"If a runner wants to build himself up for a big race, it's no good if he starts building up his arms. He can have the strongest arms in the world and they will not help him if he needs his legs to run with. And that's exactly what mankind is doing. In their ignorance, they are putting, as we may say, the least important before the most important. They are trying to satisfy their gross physical energy desires before they even think about their Spiritual Energy needs, and sooner or later, no matter what happens, they have to put this energy complex in its rightful order. If mankind has to perish terribly a million times so that he can learn this lesson, then he'll do so. If he has to starve a million times, then he'll do so. It's almost unbelievable, the absurdity of the inhabitants of this Planet. And some of us have foreseen this, just as the seers of old foresaw many things which have happened.

"When this Spiritual Energy crisis has been put right, and not before, all the physical energy man needs in his journey through evolution must come to him by Karmic Law. The knowledge how to get it must come to him then. So we have a physical energy crisis facing us today and in the years to come, purely because man has not given Spiritual Energy its right importance. Stop and think about the real sources of energy and how to use these correctly. If you do it through religion, then do it through your religion. If you do so as a non-religious person, then do it as a non-religious person. But do it! Use the vast Spiritual Energy battery which is the whole of Creation. Let it course through you; become a radiator for this and send it out to all and go through the whole process of evolution.

"There is only one reason man is on Earth: to evolve. And there is one sure way to do it—controlling Spiritual Energy. You will be gradually more and more denied the use of these lower forms of energy, your gasoline and so on, until you really turn back to the Spiritual things, and then, and only then, will you have abundance. Fortunately for all of us, Spiritual Energy does not need tremendous technical help to obtain it. All we have to do is to walk outside, throw up our arms and say one of the Twelve Blessings, and immediately Spiritual Energy starts to course through us.

"There has been an energy crisis on Earth for many centuries; it's a Spiritual Energy crisis. When that Spiritual Energy crisis is put right, the physical energy crisis will fall automatically into place. Until that Spiritual Energy crisis is put right, the physical energy crisis will become more and more severe, no matter what strides are made to solve it."

SATELLITE NO. 3

Through Their contacts with Dr. George King, the Cosmic Intelligences have introduced the most effective programme of help possible to potentize our output of Spiritual Energy on this world. They are always governed by the Law of Karma which determines just how much They can intervene in the affairs of mankind. The same Law which prevents Them from landing openly among us yet and proving Themselves to all doubters, limits the amount of help They can give us in solving the energy crisis. Because of this, They have devised a carefully crafted plan to send as much Spiritual Energy as possible to mankind. Central to this plan is the activity of a Spacecraft called Satellite No. 3, which is under the overall command of the Cosmic Master known as Mars Sector 6.

On May 28th, 1955, Satellite No. 3 started orbiting our world at regular intervals. In the same way that the Star of Bethlehem had a specialized mission to perform in bringing about the birth of the Venusian Jesus, so Satellite No. 3 has a very specialized mission around our world.

It comes into regular orbits, 1,550 miles above the surface of Earth. The dates of these orbits into the future have been released through contacts with Dr. King. During a telepathic Transmission on October 11th, 1988, Mars Sector 6 revealed that the Spiritual Push dates for the next one thousand years will be:

April 18th—May 23rd
July 5th—August 5th
September 3rd—October 9th
November 4th—December 10th

Colossal amounts of Spiritual Energy are beamed down to anyone on Earth who is ready to use it. The purpose of this energy is to potentize all selfless actions, no matter who is performing them, by a factor of 3,000 times. If you are engaged in some kind of selfless or humanitarian work during one of these periods, which are known as Magnetization Periods or Spiritual Pushes, the effect of your actions, from a Karmic point of view, will be 3,000 times greater.

This fantastic manipulation of Spiritual Energy does not only apply to people who know about these orbits, but to anyone of any religious persuasion, as well as people who would not regard themselves as religious who are engaged in humanitarian work. So delicate is the Karmic balance on this Earth as a result of the selfish behaviour of mankind, which has gone on for centuries, that the Controllers of Satellite No. 3 have to wait for actions to be performed by human beings before They, in turn, can act. When such actions are performed in Service, then They can potentize the effect of those actions 3,000 times.

Satellite No. 3 represents a combination of a science so advanced as to be beyond the comprehension, never mind belief, of most scientists on Earth, with a demonstrated religious conviction and love for all life, even alien life. Aetherius Society Members and sympathizers around the world join together to cooperate with the First and Last Hours of all Spiritual Pushes, as well as holding many special activities during them, which are designed to send out as much Spiritual Energy as possible through Prayer and Mantra. This is one definite way we can all help solve the energy crisis, and thereby save humanity from himself.

Dr. King has had the very rare honour, on more than one occasion, of actually visiting Satellite No. 3, and witnessing the complex computerized technology which performs these amazing feats of miraculous Service. He achieved this through the advanced Yogic feat of conscious astral projection.

This state is often referred to as an "out of body experience," but in Dr. King's case it was performed under full control at will. These are his words after a visit to the Third Satellite on March 23rd, 1956.

"I became immediately aware that I was in a huge room, housing a tremendous amount of beautifully

designed apparatus. The whole place was filled with a soft, exquisite radiance, more beautiful than that found in any place on Earth. The atmosphere was filled with an alluring perfume, not strong enough to be detected by the physical senses, but denotable by the reaction it had upon my etheric body. This perfume was an energy which, if concentrated upon, would bring on the deeper states of trance, regarded on Earth as Samadhi. Even though I did not really concentrate upon or tune into this perfume energy, its presence had a clearing effect upon my mind.

"In the middle of the ceiling, covering about a quarter of its huge domed surface, there was a large circular window. This was made of pure crystal, very finely ground and completely free from all flaws such as those which might be found in terrestrial glass, which would be likely to blur the images seen through it. The crystal window allowed the free passage of all Solar rays, as well as magnetic rays coming from other Planetary Bodies, which latter shone against the purple background of Space with a scintillating brilliance never observed from the surface of Earth. The huge crystal window could be made into a filter by charging it with certain energies, affecting its selection of Solar and magnetic rays. During this charging process, the crystal changed colour from a soft rose pink, to a pulsating violet, according to the selection imposed by the Operators of the Satellite.

"Beneath the huge window stood three large crystal prisms which broke up the Solar spectrum into its primary colours. Each spectrometric colour was then split into seven further shades by another large crystal which held my fascinated gaze. This huge crystal structure seemed to be about 25 to 30 feet high, shaped like a giant egg. What its physical weight must have been, I do not know—but it defied all the known laws of gravity, because it floated in space, being neither fastened to the domed ceiling nor to the metal floor of the Spacecraft.

"Slowly revolving around this great egg-shaped crystal were numerous other multi-shaped crystalline formations. These moved in slow procession from the top to the bottom in an elliptical orbit. They passed between the tip of the ovoid and the great domed roof of the Spacecraft to continue their travel down the side of it, passing between the bright metal floor and the bottom of this gigantic egg.

"The great ovoid glowed as from some internal fires, obviously radiating energies which were conditioned by 'something' within it. The primary colours of the Solar rays, broken down by the three huge prisms, were absorbed into the ovoid structure and radiated outwards, each one split up again into seven further aspects of energy. These colours I could not name, because I have never seen their equivalent on Earth. But I did notice, with great interest, that when each primary colour was broken down by the ovoid, the resultant energy seemed to flow slowly, like a kind of liquid capable of being guided through the transmitting mechanism. The latter was made of a type of metal unknown to me, in the shape of a large matrix. This matrix was formed of intricate lines of metal which ran in very finely cut channels intersecting each other at exactly 90 degree angles. In fact, I was later informed that this angle of intersection was computed so exactly that the whole matrix had to be built in Space so that the curvature of a planetary mass would not affect the precise angles of intersection! From this matrix the conditioned energies were radiated to any destination on Earth.

"The amazing scientists on the Third Satellite have, by a simple process of light manipulation, isolated the Universal Life Forces referred to by the Sages as—Prana. These subtle Pranas are the energies with which the Manipulators on the Third Satellite are flooding this dark little Planet during every Magnetization Period. They can blend and interweave them in complicated patterns and guide the resultant energies to any spot on the surface of Earth."

On December 10th, 1988, it was announced that in 1989, Satellite No. 3 would be replaced by another vehicle more sophisticated and advanced in its technology even than the first. This new craft is 12,000 feet in length, as opposed to 7,920 feet in length which the former vessel had been. Since that date it has continued to perform Spiritual Pushes using the same name of—Satellite No. 3.

This massive contribution of Spiritual Energy, in the form of both quantity and quality (vibrational rate), as well as its effect as a Karmic manipulation, is the greatest possible contribution the Gods from Space could possibly make to our world. This is far more valuable to our well-being than hundreds of UFO sightings or even landings. This is direct action on the part of the Cosmic Masters—the rest is up to us. Cooperation by mankind with Satellite No. 3, both now and in the future, is one of the main ways this world can be changed in a lasting way. It is also one of the best ways to prove to yourself that this Spacecraft exists. If you send out Spiritual power regularly during these orbits, you will start to feel the difference in power radiation inside and outside a Spiritual Push. In the words of Dr. King:

"Miracles are not performed by God for man, but by man for God."

OPERATION SPACE POWER

The transmission of energy from Satellite No. 3 is greatly enhanced by the use of radionic apparatus by The Aetherius Society. Equipment designed by Dr. King and built by Aetherius Society technicians, called Spiritual Energy Radiators, are aligned at certain times during Spiritual Pushes with the radiation of beams of Spiritual Energy from Satellite No. 3. At the present time there are two Spiritual Energy Radiators in operation, one located at the Society's American Headquarters in Hollywood, California, and the other located at the Society's European Headquarters in London, England.

Each of these Spiritual Energy Radiators operates for at least three hours a day during a Spiritual Push, making a total of six hours per day. Information supplied by a Cosmic Source has revealed that during this six hour period, no less than 12,240 Prayer Hours per day are sent through these two Spiritual machines. In theory, a Prayer Hour represents the equivalent of one hour of unselfish Prayer by one person. The intensity of the Spiritual Energy radiated by Satellite No. 3 is greater than the capacity of an ordinary person to pray on Earth, as you would expect from such an advanced Spacecraft, but the frequency level of the energy is kept at a low enough level to be usable by ordinary people on Earth.

Even more importantly, the energy is manipulated very precisely to bring the most potent result. This Mission, which is called Operation Space Power, makes an immense difference to the output of Spiritual Energy during a Spiritual Push. It acts as a Karmic manipulation to increase the amount transmitted during these Holy times.

In addition to this increased energy output during a Spiritual Push, Dr. King received a series of communications in 1987 which resulted in an additional source of millions of Prayer Hours of Spiritual Energy, which had previously been radiated through Operation Space Power, but not used by mankind. This source of energy, located in Space at a place designated "Central Control," is available both inside and outside a Spiritual Push through an arrangement with Cosmic Intelligences which will continue after Dr. King's demise. Again, the energy is radiated through one of the Society's Spiritual Energy Radiators and can be used at moments of world crisis, such as peace negotiations, earthquakes, hurricanes and so forth. This Mission, which does not depend on Satellite No. 3 being in orbit, is termed Operation Space Power II.

OPERATION PRAYER POWER

Another Mission devised by Dr. George King to help solve the energy crisis on Earth is called Operation Prayer Power. This Mission also uses technology devised by Dr. King, this time in coordination with the devotional Prayers and Mantras of Members and sympathizers of The Aetherius Society through-out the world. The energy source for this Mission is the invocation of Spiritual Power by highly trained Prayer and Mantra practitioners in a beautifully balanced ritual. But instead of sending the energy out directly to the world, it is stored in what is known as a Prayer Battery. This Battery is a piece of physical equipment, similar in size to the ordinary chemical battery you would find in a car. It is constructed from radionic materials, i.e. materials which conduct Spiritual Energies, such as high quality gold and quartz crystals.

The principle of Operation Prayer Power, which combines perfectly the essence of both science and religion, is that hundreds of hours of energy invoked by Prayer and Mantra can be stored. This can then be used at a time of crisis or great need. In order to quantify the amount of energy contained in a Battery at any one time, an assessment is made, both of the quality and quantity of energy put out by each prayer in turn as their hand is held in front of the aperture of the Battery. This follows exactly the same principle as Spiritual Healing where, through the laying on of hands, energy is transferred through the psychic centres in the palms of the hands. In Operation Prayer Power the motive is mass healing rather than individual healing. The energy is transmitted through the palm of the hand of the person praying and into the Prayer Battery, where it is stored for future use. While an individual is praying, all the others present chant sacred Mantras and channel their energy towards the person praying, through whom it is transmitted into the Battery.

The Prayers used are taken from *The Twelve Blessings* and the Mantras are ancient Sanskrit sound systems, perfectly attuned to the environment, which invoke natural energies from the ethers around. As well as calculating the exact amount of time spent in prayer, the quality is taken into account by specially trained Prayer Assessors who designate the performance of each Prayer into a category such as A, A+, or AA+.

Using calculations given by a Cosmic Intelligence during a close encounter with Dr. King, timekeepers are able to allocate the exact amount of energy invoked. A high quality Prayer will invoke a greater amount of energy than a lower quality Prayer. All Prayers do not have an equal effect or potency—hence the need for assessment. It depends on the power of invocation achieved by each prayer and the degree to which they are able to act as a channel for the energy invoked by the Mantra team.

It is almost impossible for any religion on Earth to get 1,000 people together, exactly when you need them during a world crisis, to pray with full intensity and concentration for one hour. However, with energy stored in Prayer Batteries, The

Aetherius Society is in a position to release 1,000 or more Prayer Hours exactly when it is needed. Such a release is performed through one of the Spiritual Energy Radiators, in direct cooperation with the Cosmic Masters. During a Spiritual Push, a regular release of this energy is manipulated by the extraterrestrial scientists on Satellite No. 3 Who know exactly where on the Earth energy is needed at any given time. Regular Operation Prayer Power discharges, as they are called, are performed both in London and Los Angeles.

Operation Prayer Power is currently being performed in London and Barnsley, England, in Los Angeles and Michigan, U.S.A., and in Auckland, New Zealand. Operation Prayer Power pilgrimages are also regularly held at Holdstone Down in North Devon, which is regarded by the Society as a Holy Mountain. These are attended by up to 200 Members and sympathizers of The Aetherius Society. There is no reason at all why this Mission should not spread and be performed throughout the world and hence make a massive difference to solving the energy crisis on our world.

As well as regular discharges in cooperation with Satellite No. 3, Operation Prayer Power discharges are also performed to meet specific crises when they occur. In some of these, it is possible to assess the situation in these crisis areas both before and after the event. Here are just a few examples:

July 21st–22nd, 1974

Between 9.30 p.m. and 12.50 p.m., an Operation Prayer Power Battery in London was discharged. Some 542 Prayer Hours were released during this manipulation. At the time, a vicious war between the Turks and the Greeks was being waged over the island of Cyprus, which threatened the peace of the whole Middle East and possibly the world. The Spiritual Energy was directed to the peacemakers gathered in the United Nations in New York, as well as on Cyprus, under the threat of the Greek government of an all-out war with Turkey. Within hours after the Battery had been discharged, a first ceasefire in the war was accepted by both sides. Further, the Cyprus regime, headed by terrorist gunmen, was forced to quit and a few hours later the seven years of inhuman rule by the military dictatorship of Greece by the so-called 'Colonels' also came to an end.

April 23rd, 1981

Three hundred and sixty-three Prayer Hours from an Aetherius Society Prayer Battery, and 1,046 Prayer Hours from a Battery of the Great White Brotherhood, were released to Poland. After this discharge, against all the predictions of political experts, the Soviet Union decided not to invade Poland, despite the anti-communist feelings there. This was unprecedented in the history of the Soviet block up to that date. Poland was later to become the catalyst for the downfall of communism throughout eastern Europe.

October 30th–November 29th, 1983

On October 30th, 1983, there was a huge earthquake in north-east Turkey, measuring more than 6 points on the Richter Scale. Tragically, around 2,000 were killed and many others injured and made homeless. Between October 30th and November 3rd, The Aetherius Society discharged 692 Prayer Hours to victims and to rescue teams in the area. Additional releases of 2,700 Prayer Hours by advanced Masters using their own equipment also took place between October 30th and November 29th to rescue teams in the area of the original and subsequent earthquakes. On November 6th, another earthquake in western Turkey, measuring 4 points on the Richter Scale, caused damage to buildings in a number of villages, but this time, there were no fatalities. On November 18th, a larger earthquake, measuring 5.6 points on the Richter Scale, again struck eastern Turkey in the Erzincan Province, 200 kilometers from the area which had been struck on October 30th. Remarkably, there were no deaths and only five people were reported as having been slightly injured. This difference between the effects of the first earthquake and the subsequent two was staggering.

September 19th–21st, 1985

Operation Prayer Power discharges were made to Mexico City after an earthquake of 8.5 Richter Scale magnitude, which consisted of 1,250 Prayer Hours from The Aetherius Society and 8,626 Prayer Hours from the Great White Brotherhood. Additionally, there was a release of 11,220 Prayer Hours from Satellite No. 3 through the Spiritual Energy Radiator. Mexico City is the largest city in the world in terms of population, with over 17 million people, and is the most densely populated area on this Planet. Despite this, only around 7,000 people were killed, far less than might have been expected. There were numerous reports of miracles, such as Mexican labourers, who often worked 14 to 18 hours without rest for no pay, unexpectedly finding people amidst the rubble when many would have given up, and so on. Expert international rescue teams were also brought into the area. A potentially destructive tidal wave which had been forecast did not materialize.

March 16th, 1986

There was a discharge of Operation Prayer Power energy from the Society's American Headquarters to alleviate "Tornado Watch" conditions on the west coast of the United States. A total of 350 Prayer Hours was discharged, after which, tornadoes did not materialize and the storm was not nearly as severe as had been forecast. In fact, even though storms were predicted to continue, the following morning, the Sun was shining from a blue, cloudless sky, much to everyone's amazement.

September 16th, 1988

Three hundred Prayer Hours were discharged to alleviate the predicted devastation from "Hurricane Gilbert." A further 12,900 Prayer Hours were released by the Great White Brotherhood and other Masters around the Earth. Despite forecasts that this hurricane would move northward through Texas, it did not, but instead travelled into a relatively uninhabited area, and gradually reduced in power. There were many reports of heroic deeds and a massive relief effort was mounted.

January 6th–8th, 1993

Two separate discharges of over 550 Prayer Hours each were made following the oil spill of the "Braer" tanker in the Shetlands, Scotland. Despite dire warnings of ecological disaster, the final death toll reported in the press on June 16th, 1993, was only 1,542 birds, six otters and no whales. This was in contrast to the "Exxon Valdez" spill in Alaska during 1989 when 300,000 black guillemots alone died, and this spill was only half the amount of oil released by the "Braer" tanker. Some reports described the ecological recovery in the Shetlands as miraculous.

In some of these cases you will have seen reference to additional discharges of energy by the Great White Brotherhood and other Masters. In accordance with the Law of Karma, they cannot intervene in terrestrial affairs beyond a certain point. They are literally waiting for our actions to manipulate this

Law, which then allows their intervention. Our discharges act virtually as triggers for them to send their power and energy, which is, of course, far greater and more effective than ours.

When Dr. King first devised this Mission, which was inaugurated on June 30th, 1973, on Holdstone Down in England, he dedicated it to ecology. Some of the examples referred to illustrate the success of this Operation in altering weather conditions and other ecological effects. This is because the ecological balance around our world is maintained by the living nature spirits known as the "Devas". These are not just fairies and elves, but can be massively powerful forces of nature, referred to as Devic Lords, who are responsible for controlling the tides of the oceans and major weather conditions around the Earth. They manipulate the energies that they receive from mankind, for better or for worse, to bring about the ecological balance we have deserved. They work in total cooperation with the Law of Karma in doing so. By sending out power and energy to these great forces, we can alter and improve the natural ecological balance of our Earth, which is one of the most pressing of all the challenges which face us in these days.

To solve all the problems on Earth we must use, to the fullest possible extent, the energy which is available to us. In the quotation which opens this chapter, Mars Sector 6 referred to the colossal energy available to all mankind from Satellite No. 3 during a Spiritual Push. He continued this Cosmic Transmission, which was entitled "From Freewill to Freedom" and delivered on February 28th, 1960, in New York, with the following words:

"If your motives be pure, and we know them exactly, then the energy will be given unto you. If your motive be not pure, look not towards this source for energy, for none will be forthcoming."

Dr. George King, Commander-in-Chief of Operation Prayer Power, coordinates Prayer Energy releases in cooperation with the Great White Brotherhood and other Cosmic Forces.

Dr. George King manipulates Prayer Energy into the Battery at the inauguration of Operation Prayer Power in America, at Lake Powell, Utah, 1973.

CHAPTER SIX

Spiritual Ecology

"Blessed is She, Who, in sacrifice,
has made a Space refuge for you all."

— *the Master Jesus*

MOTHER EARTH

From his earliest contacts with advanced Intelligences from other worlds, Dr. George King received communications about the vital importance of the Mother Earth as a living Entity. He also promoted the importance of what we now call ecology—indeed he championed this cause many years before it became fashionable.

Most people who are committed to ecology give as their motive the preservation of the human race and future generations on our world. But there are an increasing number who go further than this and speak about the Earth as a living Being. People are starting to promote the cause of ecology, not just for the sake of the human race, but more for the sake of the Planet upon which we live.

Like so many so-called "discoveries," there is nothing new whatsoever about regarding the Mother Earth as a living Being. The ancient Greeks used to call Her Gaia, the goddess of Earth, or as their "Hymn to Gaia" expresses it, "mother of the gods, bride of starry Heaven." This Hymn, written over 2,500 years ago, was sung or spoken as a prelude to a festival. It begins in the following way:

"Gaia, mother of all,
The foundation, the oldest one,
I shall sing to Earth.
She feeds everything in the world.

115

**Whoever you are,
Whether you move upon her sacred ground
Or whether you go along the paths of the sea,
You that fly, it is She
Who nourishes you from her treasure-store."**

Concepts of the Mother Earth go back thousands of years. The Indo-European name for the Goddess Earth was Plataea, literally the "Broad One." So-called primitive civilizations from Africa to the Americas, to the Antipodes, to Asia, to the Celts, who spoke about the Earth as a living female Intelligence, were more advanced in this one Spiritual realization than the scientists, imperialists and Christian missionaries who imposed their own, far more limited dogmas upon many of them. It is, therefore, heart-warming to see a gradual appreciation of the Earth as a living Being re-emerging in modern times.

On July 4th, 1994, the United States of America awarded the Liberty Medal to the Czech President, Vaclav Havel. In his speech of acceptance he made the following statement:

"According to the Gaia Hypothesis, we are parts of a greater whole. Our destiny is not dependent merely on what we do for ourselves, but also on what we do for Gaia as a whole. If we endanger Her, She will dispense with us in the interests of a higher value—life itself."

In recent years, a number of scientists have developed this so-called Gaia Hypothesis by proving that the Earth is indeed a living organism. This idea is not completely new to modern science. James Hutton, often regarded as the father of geology, said in 1785, in a lecture in Edinburgh: "I consider the Earth to be a superorganism, and its proper study is by physiology." This was a revolutionary concept in his day and, not surprisingly, was by and large ignored for almost two centuries. However, the findings of modern science and the emergence of ecology as an accepted concept have led increasing numbers to see the Earth as a living organism. They do so on the basis that life on Earth would be highly improbable without some extraordinary manipulation, which defies normal geophysical principles, taking place.

The quantities of methane and oxygen gases in the atmosphere, which keep going the balanced conditions necessary for life as we know it, are very small. According to the scientist James Lovelock, who was awarded the first Amsterdam Prize for the Environment by the Royal Netherlands Academy of Arts and Sciences in 1990, the probability of both these gases being constantly produced in the right mixture to keep the Earth's atmosphere conducive to life, was infinitesimal. He estimated it to be improbable for this to occur by at least 100 orders of magnitude (10 to the power of 100). When the whole chemical composition of the atmosphere and the climate around Earth are taken into account, he estimated the probability of such conditions as being as unlikely as that of a driver who has been blindfolded surviving unscathed during traffic in the rush hour.

So whether you turn to ancient mystical beliefs or whether you look at the increased findings of modern science, there is no question that the Earth lives. She is not an inanimate lump of rock which we cherish purely as we might cherish the possession of a home, but a vast, living Intelligence. The Mother Earth has provided for us and allows us to gain experience in the only way we are capable of doing so. In fact, the more you study the facts about the Planet on which we live, the more you realize how fortunate we are and how much She must have suffered on our behalf. Spiritual ecology is not primarily a concern for the continuance of the human race, crucial though that is; it is more a concern for the Planet Herself Who is more important even than the race which inhabits Her.

In "The Twelve Blessings," the Master Jesus makes the following heart-wrenching statement:

"Blessed is the Logos of this Earth for She shineth like a Sun doth shine. Yet—of purpose—She hideth this Light beneath the bushel of a material form, which renders unto man, sustenance."

In other words, Her material existence is preserved in its current form, not so much for Her benefit, but for the benefit of mankind. She does not need to exist in the way that She does. She could be a far more radiant Being, but this would change the atmospheric belt on a physical level around the Earth, and we would not be able to inhabit this Planet. It is for our benefit that She hides Her Light beneath the bushel of a material form at a low enough vibratory rate to cater for mankind's needs.

Interplanetary Masters from other worlds inhabit Planets like Jupiter and Venus, which some scientists tell us are uninhabitable, because they are able to exist at higher frequencies of energy output. They do not exist on the basic physical level that we do, but radiate a much higher frequency of vibration. This means that the Planets on which They live are not so limited by the races who inhabit Them. The Mother Earth is in a different position. She has to withhold Her true Spiritual stature in order to allow us to exist. In this respect, She is a much more advanced version of those great Avatars Who visited this Earth and suffered to help mankind, such as the Master Jesus, the Lord Buddha, Shri Krishna and others Who rightfully belonged in the bodies of Gods at a much higher level of evolution than our physical world, but forsook this to live among us here.

Very few people in history have had even a glimpse of the true Light of the Mother Earth or any part of it. One person who has is Dr. George King, and he describes his experience of seeing a part of the living Flame of the Mother Earth in his book *Visit To The Logos Of Earth*. In order to get a real appreciation of this experience you do need to study and meditate on this book. The following paragraph, however, summarizes the effect this outstanding experience had upon Dr. King:

"I wanted to weep—and I did so.
"I have seen kind deeds and heard of kinder deeds, but never a deed as compassionate as this. Here She was, confined to Her self-imposed prison of limitation so that you and I and billions more of us could work our way through our present experience cycle. All She had to do was to use Her stupendous inner powers and few of us would be able to exist on or around this Planet; but those few would not be obsessed, like the majority, by greed and hate and jealousy which, when expressed, results in war and murder and pillage, and untold damage to Her beautiful body."

Through helping the ecological balance at every etheric level, humanity, too, is helped, raised and spiritualized. From a Karmic point of view, the more that mankind does for the Mother Earth, the better his position Spiritually and in every other way. By drilling for oil, releasing so-called controlled nuclear explosions, and by pollution in every form, we are not cooperating with Her, Who has made our material existence possible at great cost to Herself.

THE INITIATION OF EARTH
The New Age movement as a whole has missed out, for the most part, on the main point about it. It is not just a New Age for mankind—but even more for the Earth as a living Planet. The New Age will start to dawn during the Aquarian Age, but will last

way beyond this next 2,000-year cycle. Many people argue about the exact date of the start of the New Age. There are numerous theories about this drawn from astrology and other predictions. The true answer is that there will be an overlapping period between the Piscean Age, which started 2000 years ago, and the Aquarian Age. But if one was to take one date from which the New Age started to dawn it would be July 8th, 1964.

The most important event in recorded history took place on this day, namely, **The Primary Initiation of Earth.** Massive Spiritual Powers of colossal force and extremely high frequency were radiated by and through the Gods from Space to the Mother Earth as a living Entity. These powers now lie dormant within Her and will be gradually released, thereby raising all the vibrations around this Earth and bringing into manifestation the prophesied New Age of enlightenment, peace and brotherhood. It will virtually be heaven on Earth. The New Age is not so much about us, as it is about Her. It is for us to make the change necessary to enjoy Her Initiation.

All Members of The Aetherius Society devote themselves to a day of Prayer on July 8th every year, in deference to the Planet upon Whom we all depend for sustenance, and something even more important than this—experience. This is Her day and therefore, for Society Members, the most important in the calendar.

OPERATION STARLIGHT

Before the Primary Initiation of Earth, two Missions were performed by Dr. George King in cooperation with the Cosmic Masters, which directly affected the Planet. A total of 19 mountains around the world were charged with Spiritual Power from Cosmic Sources between July 23rd, 1958, and August 23rd, 1961, in a Mission called Operation Starlight. On every occasion except one, Dr. King was required personally to climb these mountains so that a charge of energy could be radiated through him. He was, if you like, a Karmic "anchor point." Whenever a manipulation is made by the Gods from Space for the benefit of this Earth, Karma has to be manipulated by one or more human beings. If it was not, direct Divine Intervention would have taken place, contravening the ancient all-pervasive Law of God.

A full list of all the Holy Mountains charged during Operation Starlight is as follows:

Dr. George King, atop Mt. Ramshead, Australia, immediately after completing Phase 14 on December 5th, 1960.

Holdstone Down, Devon, England
Brown Willy, Cornwall, England
Ben Hope, The Highlands, Scotland
Creag-An-Leth-Chain, Grampian, Scotland
The Old Man of Coniston, Cumbria, England
Pen-Y-Fan, Powys, Wales
Carnedd Llywelyn, Gwynedd, Wales
Kinderscout, Derbyshire, England
Yes Tor, Devon, England
Mount Baldy, California, U.S.A.
Mount Tallac, California, U.S.A.
Mount Adams, New Hampshire, U.S.A.
Castle Peak, Colorado, U.S.A.
Mount Kosciusko, New South Wales, Australia
Mount Ramshead, New South Wales, Australia
Mount Wakefield, Southern Island, New Zealand
Mount Kilimanjaro, Tanzania, Africa
Mount Madrigerfluh, Switzerland
Le Nid d'Aigle, France

Because this Mission had to be completed within a certain time-frame for Karmic reasons, and because of the mystical significance of the British Isles as a region of the Mother Earth, no less than nine of these mountains are in England, Scotland and Wales.

These mountains are now Power sources. In the New Age, it will not just be a question of worshipping in Temples, Churches and other buildings, it will also be a time to worship beneath the open dome of the sky above us. You can go to any one of these 19 mountains and send out some of their power through the practice of Prayer, Mantra or Healing to others around the world. The Aetherius Society manufactures Holy Shapes containing stones from these mountains so that Members can potentize their Spiritual exercises and Yoga practices at home. Temples of The Aetherius Society have large, specially manufactured Holy Crosses, each containing all 19 of these Holy Stones.

These Holy Mountains are batteries of power which all people can use, regardless of their religious beliefs. You could be a believer in any religion or none, and still gain the benefit of climbing one of these Holy Mountains, providing your motive is to send out Spiritual Power for the benefit of others. Every year The Aetherius Society arranges mass pilgrimages to several of these mountains, during which pilgrims can experience for themselves the great energies which are there.

You might say that such pilgrimages are not really Spiritual ecology because they are for the benefit of mankind and you would be right. The Holy Mountains were charged as an answer to the Spiritual Energy crisis which exists on Earth. It was foreseen by the Cosmic Masters that it would be necessary to leave certain power sources for men and women of good heart to use to send out Spiritual Energy at this time of dire need and into our future. A Karmic agent was needed to make this miracle possible, and Dr. George King was chosen for this task, assisted in most cases by the small teams who climbed with him. An ordinary person can climb one of these 19 Holy Mountains and send out as much power to the world as could an Adept in the science of Yoga.

OPERATION BLUEWATER

The other Mission which commenced before the Initiation of Earth was Operation Bluewater. This was a Mission of true Spiritual ecology—it was performed for the benefit of the Earth Herself, thereby benefiting the ecological balance of the world and preventing catastrophic meteorological disasters and a devastating earthquake, which were due at the time.

Performed between July 11th, 1963, and November 29th, 1964, Operation Bluewater required Dr. George King and a small team to take a boat out off Newport Beach on the California coast. The principle of this Mission was the same as that of giving Spiritual Healing to human beings. Just as we have chakras, or psychic centres, so does the Planet on which we live. In Spiritual Healing, the healer radiates natural energies through his or her palms of the hands into the psychic centres of their patient. In Operation Bluewater the Cosmic Masters radiated Cosmic Energies through radionic apparatus which was taken by boat over a psychic centre located nearly 2,000 feet beneath the sea in the San Pedro Channel. This brought balance to the Earth, just as healing does to a patient, preventing mass flooding and other dire consequences which would otherwise have occurred.

The Aetherius Society takes practical metaphysics from a purely individual level to a global level—and Operation Bluewater was a classic example of this. The presence of Dr. King as Primary Terrestrial Mental Channel, in communication with extraterrestrial Beings at the same time as he maneuvered the 37-foot boat, was an essential Karmic manipulation which made this Divine Intervention permissible. This is true Spiritual ecology. Without Operation Bluewater, the Earth would have had to make other adjustments which would have had cataclysmic results in certain parts of the world, especially the west coast of America.

OPERATION SUNBEAM

Operation Starlight and Operation Bluewater were given as Missions to Dr. King by the Cosmic Masters. From these, he was inspired to invent Operation Sunbeam, the world's greatest ecological Mission, which is being performed now and will continue to be performed in the future. In Operation Sunbeam, high frequency Spiritual Energies are radiated into several psychic centres of the Mother Earth. To perform this Mission two essential attributes are required: one is advanced occult knowledge to identify the location of these psychic centres, and the other is a source of high enough frequency energy to be compatible with and acceptable for the Mother Earth. Using the same principle as Operation Bluewater—of radiating Cosmic Energies into a psychic centre of Earth—Dr. King devised Operation Sunbeam in 1966, since when it has expanded and advanced greatly. He has personally discovered several psychic centres of Earth, which are used in Operation Sunbeam today.

The other main requirement of a source capable of radiating compatible energies for a Planetary Being was met by his contacts with the Gods from Space. Advanced Masters from other worlds, using energies contained in the Holy Mountains, or even from other Planets, are able to direct this energy through equipment devised by Dr. King, so that it is channelled at certain specific times into psychic centres of Earth. As with certain other Missions, Operation Sunbeam is a combination of the highest possible religious devotion with practical scientific technological apparatus. In Operation Sunbeam, energy is not sent for the use of mankind, but for the use of the Mother Earth.

The Society does not claim to be the only group of people on Earth to send out prayers, love and devotion to the Planet on Whom we all depend—far from it. Rituals have been observed through the ages by any number of tribal and religious groups. However, in Operation Sunbeam, because of the source of the energy, and the direction of it through apparatus into psychic centres of Earth, energy is uniquely offered to the Planet in a way which is acceptable to Her. Wonderful as the rites of worshippers of the Mother Earth through the ages have been, the energy has not gone directly to the Planet, because of its quality and its lack of direction. It has done great good at a natural level in helping the nature spirits with positive benign energy which they can then use to affect meteorological and other conditions around the Planet, but it is not of direct benefit to the Planet Herself. That is why Operation Sunbeam is the highest

form of Spiritual expression. Not because of the people performing it, nor even because of the equipment used. The people
who set the equipment up are providing an essential Karmic
manipulation. It could undoubtedly be better performed without
any human cooperators or physical apparatus from a purely
technical point of view, because it could be directed by the
Cosmic Masters much more effectively without us. But this
Karmic balance is as essential in Operation Sunbeam as it was in
Operation Starlight for Dr. King and a team to physically climb
the Holy Mountains of the world, and in Operation Bluewater for
Dr. King and a crew to be over a psychic centre at sea.

The Mother Earth is, in the words of the Master Jesus, "hid-
ing Her Light beneath the bushel of a material form," but will
not always do so. This Light will gradually be released as the
New Age dawns more fully upon the Earth. There will be a revi-
talization of all Spiritual thought and action—and this is
already starting to take place. There is an increasing interest in
the mysticism of religion. Today, more and more people are
questioning the religions into which they were born. They want
to know the "why" of life, and treat Spiritual activities as an
integral part of their life, not as something to just satisfy a troubled conscience once a week on Sunday morning, the Sabbath,
or whatever the case may be.

ECOLOGICAL MISSIONS

In order to allow a balanced release of energy from this Earth
into the atmosphere of the world in a controlled manner, two
other Missions have been performed by the Masters. The first of
these, called The Saturn Mission, involved Dr. King being over
two psychic centres of Earth on a boat. The two centres he used
were Loch Ness in Scotland and Lake Powell in Utah, U.S.A.
Again, the energy for this Mission was provided by Cosmic
Intelligences Who were able to radiate the required vibratory
level to bring stabilization and balance to the Earth. This ener-

gy, mingling directly with energy from the Earth Herself, radiated in the zone of a terrestrial psychic centre, brings balance to the physical realm, thereby preventing catastrophes and ecological disasters.

As the name suggests, this Mission comes under the control of Spiritual Beings from Saturn. It started in 1981 and has continued up to the present day and will continue into the future. As with all the manipulations performed by the Gods from Space, The Saturn Mission is designed to remedy the shortage and imbalance in Spiritual Energy around the Earth. This Mission has two main results: to bring world peace and to help the elemental forces, or devas, who control the weather and other natural conditions around the Earth.

The other Mission, which is also designed to bring devic stabilization and a raising of the vibrations in the ethers around the Earth, is known as Operation Earth Light. It was devised by Dr. George King originally, but it is performed by the Masters of Earth Who form the Spiritual Hierarchy of Earth. These Members of the Great White Brotherhood were acutely aware of the need for power stabilization centres around the Earth and, under the direction of the holy Lord Babaji, Their Spiritual Leader, are ready, willing and extremely capable of providing them. This Mission, Operation Earth Light, began in 1990 and will continue into the future. It allows the Mother Earth to gradually release some of the massive powers given to Her during Her Initiation in a way which is beneficial to all life upon Earth.

SPIRITUAL ECOLOGY

It is very hard to do justice to the contribution to Spiritual ecology which has been made by Dr. King and The Aetherius Society in cooperation with the Gods from Space. The fact that many may disbelieve it is irrelevant to the results. Recognition is, after all, more important for the recognizer than it is for the thing recognized. When mankind really starts to appreciate the significance of Spiritual ecology and the way in which it can be performed effectively, in cooperation with the Masters of this Earth and beyond, the New Age will be upon us.

The combination of Operation Sunbeam, in which colossal Cosmic Energies are radiated to the Mother Earth as a Karmic manipulation, and The Saturn Mission and Operation Earth Light, in which energies are radiated from the Mother Earth in balance, is a phenomenal force for terrestrial balance. It is addressing the Spiritual Energy crisis more surely than any other method, because it is dealing directly with the main Karmic problem, namely, our misuse and maltreatment of the Planet on which we live. It has to be pointed out that even among Masters of Yoga, Dr. King is rare indeed in his devotion to the Planet on which he has lived. And this devotion is not expressed so much in theory, or even Prayer, though he has done both of those things numerous times. It is expressed above all through practical, scientific Missions which he has personally devised.

It is not by chance that many reliable prophets have been proved wrong. They warned of dire natural catastrophes during this period of history and they were correct. There has been an increase in severe weather conditions and turbulent geological conditions over the last few decades. But the casualties have been described by independent observers in many of these occasions as miraculously low. It is largely because of Spiritual ecology that this is so. Prophecy should only be used as a guide to what will happen unless we make certain changes. It should never be regarded as unalterable fate. This applies just as much at a global level as it does at an individual level.

The healing Prayers and sacred Mantras performed throughout the world for the benefit of mankind can certainly help the human race and do affect our weather conditions, but they cannot deal sufficiently with the Karmic imbalance we have created in our relationship with the Planet on which we live. It is only through Missions which practice true Spiritual ecology that major steps have been taken to redress the horrendous imbalance we have created.

The Master Jesus stated in the Seventh Blessing:

"As yet, man, She has borne you. I request most strongly NOW—that you do not take such for granted. She has not, as yet, demanded that you change —or leave."

Spiritual ecology is that vital. It is vital for the sake of the Planet, and for the continuance of mankind's opportunity to reside on this Planet. This is the crux of why the Cosmic Masters have seen fit to form an organization like The Aetherius Society at this historic time in the evolution of humanity, and why They have decided to give Their wisdom to mankind now, regardless of whether he is ready to receive it. For centuries, mystics, occultists and practitioners of the true science of Yoga, withheld their sacred knowledge from all who were not ready to receive it. It would have been necessary to prove your worth, through severe tests if necessary, before you could be initiated into the higher truths. There was not the urgency then that there is now.

The change has come, not just because of the nuclear threat, though that is reason enough. It has come even more because of the Initiation of Earth and the gradual release of these initiating energies by the Earth. This is causing a raising of consciousness and a pressure on all the people who reside here. For many this is having a beneficial effect. Those who resist it are behaving more extremely in negative ways, such as violence, fanaticism and so on. A change will come to this Planet in the light of Her Initiation. Can we cooperate with this change and inherit the prophesied Heaven on Earth? That depends on us and whether we are willing to pick up the pearls which have been cast before us in these days.

Dr. George King during a Phase of The Saturn Mission, aboard his boat "Phantom," Lake Powell, Utah.

CHAPTER SEVEN

The Pearls are Cast

"In these days the pearls are cast."

— *Mars Sector 6*

CASTING THE PEARLS

"Give not that which is holy unto the dogs, neither cast ye your pearls before swine, lest they trample them under their feet, and turn again and rend you." So said Jesus during the Sermon on the Mount, according to St. Matthew, Chapter 7, Verse 6. When He gave this famous teaching, He was only reiterating a long held doctrine from the mystery schools and ashrams of old. Indeed, Jesus went further than any of His predecessors in reaching the masses, particularly given the communication limitations of those days. Most of the people He taught were not able to read or write and yet Jesus and His apostles managed to spread the message of Christianity over a vast geographic area.

In many ways Jesus was ahead of His time and was laying the foundations for the New Age approach by spreading great Truths to the public at large. But even He realized that certain restrictions should be imposed upon the spreading of these Teachings. Even then it was still not correct to place pearls of wisdom before those who completely lacked appreciation of them. Now even that has changed. For the reasons outlined a new urgency exists on our world. There is no longer time to wait or to be concerned whether people are truly ready to receive the great wisdom which is now being made available, not just to the advanced initiate, but to the ordinary man, woman and child as well. These are the days of the prophecies.

CHANGING THE PROPHECIES

It can be seen from everything written in this book so far that we are at the most critical period in our history. Indeed, this idea is not unique to The Aetherius Society's beliefs; it conforms to mystical teaching in general. Nor is it just because of the year 2000 A.D.. It goes much further than this.

The parallels between different schools of religion and philosophy are staggering. From the Book of Revelations' warning of devastating wars, natural disasters and Armageddon, followed by the coming of Christ Who will rule for 1,000 years; to Hesiod in the 8th century B.C., saying that in the final days there would be warfare and social upheaval, leading Zeus to destroy mankind for his wickedness; to the ancient Mayans believing that our current age would come to an end on December 21st, 2012—very close to the New Age period.

Hindu scribes spoke of the age of Kali Yuga, a Dark Age which precedes the Golden Age. One of the oldest sacred texts in India, the Vishnu Purana, describes the latter days of Kali Yuga vividly:

"The causes of devotion will be confined to physical well-being; the only bond between the sexes will be passion; the only road to success will be the lie.

"The Earth will be honoured for its material treasures only.

"The priestly vestments will be a substitute for the quality of the priest.

"A simple absolution will mean purification; the race will be incapable of producing divine birth.

"Men will ask: what authority have the traditional tests?...

"Every way of life will be equally promiscuous for all."

Does this prophecy made thousands of years ago remind you of anything? It certainly sounds like the period we are now in.

The Old Testament prophet Joel reported in Chapter 20, Verses 30-31 of his Book, the following "words of God":

"And I will show wonders in the heavens and in the Earth, blood and fire, and pillars of smoke. The Sun shall be turned into darkness, and the moon into blood, before the great and the terrible day of the Lord come."

Again, this is a prophecy which indicates apocalyptic terror, resembling a nuclear holocaust, followed by a great "day of the Lord."

Mother Shipton, a seer from the Middle Ages who predated Nostradamus, is claimed to have said:

**"When women dress like men and trousers wear,
And cut off all their locks of hair,
When pictures look alive with movements free,
When ships like fishes swim beneath the sea,
When men outstripping birds can soar the sky,
Then half the world, deep drenched in blood, shall die."**

It is hard to ignore these words attributed to a prophetess who apparently foretold televisions, submarines and aircraft at a time when such things would have seemed completely impossible and confined to the realms of sheer magic. She is said to have also forecast dire catastrophe befalling the world at the end of the 20th century.

The key thing is how we respond to these prophecies. The Aetherius Society is working to change the negative aspects of them in cooperation with the Gods from Space, and to prepare for the positive New World which lies ahead. Dr. King has revealed that even Armageddon has already been fought and won by the Forces of Light as reported in Aetherius Society teachings.

Far from giving in to negative foreboding, by studying the Cosmic message you can see that there is greater opportunity now than has ever been offered to the people of Earth before. That, too, was foretold, and that is the real reason why the pearls have been cast before all mankind at this time, regardless of how prepared he is to receive them.

JOIN YOUR SHIP

One such pearl was cast by the Master Aetherius on August 22nd, 1964, in a Cosmic Transmission entitled: "Join Your Ship." This Transmission was delivered through Dr. King in deep Samadhic trance in front of a public audience in Los Angeles. The following are extracts:

"Today—NOW, your Spiritual actions will be more fruitful than ever they have been before in your TOTAL HISTORY. Today, NOW, Karma will be balanced quicker than ever before in your TOTAL HISTORY. Whether that Karma applies to you as an individual, as a member of a race, a country or the whole mass of humanity, this will be so. Therefore, because this is so, it is only logical to conclude that NEVER BEFORE was Spiritual action as essential as it is now...

"We are revealing these things to you now so that those who can think, do so. So that those who, like many of you, are floating about in the winds of indecision, make BOLD your decision to JOIN YOUR CHOSEN SHIP to make the journey over the rough seas, so that, when you are aboard this chosen ship, you may receive the Truth which will eventually set you free from limitation, so that you may take your rightful place in the world and so guide others who are heading for the rocks of involution.

"You have a very interesting time ahead. You have a time ahead of great accomplishment—or the greatest frustration you have ever known since you came to Terra. Please take my advice. I am many millions of years older than you are in Cosmic matters. This is your key term: JOIN YOUR SHIP. Choose it very carefully, make it the most serious choice of your life—then—JOIN IT."

In this short extract the Master Aetherius is revealing a change in the Karmic Law Itself. Karmic factors are constantly in flux depending on the overall effects of thoughts and actions. Because of the crucial stage in evolution that mankind has reached, and even more because of the changes taking place within the Planet Herself, which the Master refers to as Terra, Karma can be balanced quicker than ever before. This means that Spiritual actions—in other words, actions performed for the benefit of others—will be more potent than ever before because they are needed more now than ever before.

The Master Aetherius is urging mankind in this Transmission to commit himself – to come off the fence of indecision and make a choice and stand by it. Never has this been more urgent than it is now. World conditions alone would indicate this, never mind the Cosmic factors already explained in this book.

It was considered a Chinese curse to say "may you live in interesting times." The Taoist philosophy was one of stillness, peace and changelessness, but then the goal of that philosophy was to attain a higher state of consciousness regardless of outside events. The goal today is certainly to attain a higher state of consciousness but not regardless of outside events. When the Master Aetherius talks of "a very interesting time ahead," He is certainly implying the dangers which could potentially envelop the Earth, but He is also talking of the great potential for Spiritual accomplishment which is the other side of the same Karmic coin. In his commentary on this text, Dr. George King made the following call to action:

"In this Transmission, the Master Aetherius is making a definite appeal for people to choose their path, choose their organization *and join it with all their hearts, their minds and their souls.*"

Although The Aetherius Society does not preach a "one and only way" doctrine or attempt to convert anyone to our beliefs, it is obvious that Members of The Aetherius Society have chosen this organization because they believe it is the most effective way of changing this world for the good, and of advancing themselves Spiritually. Once you realize that lasting solutions can only be brought at a Spiritual Energy level, you turn to the organization that you feel can remedy this situation the most effectively, as well as give you a path to your own evolution. These two factors are dovetailed perfectly one into the other, because the more effective Service you give to the world as a whole, the more powerfully you manipulate your own Karma, and hence the quicker you evolve back to God.

THE MASTER COG

The Master Aetherius made it clear that The Aetherius Society has a unique role in the world today in an earlier Cosmic Transmission delivered on April 1st, 1961, entitled "The Master Cog." He made the following statements:

"There are many so-called metaphysical organizations upon Terra. There is not one, My dear friends, there is not one which will be called upon to do a bigger task than the one to which you are fortunate to belong ...

"The Aetherius Society is an essential part, an essential cog in the great Cosmic Plan. It is the

*'Master Cog' which is being driven by a Cosmic bat-
tery. If this cog breaks, the battery cannot discharge itself correctly and a new cog will have to be
hand-moulded."*

From this you can see that The Aetherius Society is just as
much a commando force, as far as the Cosmic Masters are concerned, as it is a religious organization. It has been given
Missions to be performed during the lifetime of Dr. King and
beyond. Operation Prayer Power, Operation Sunbeam, the
Spiritual Pushes, the Holy Mountains charged in Operation
Starlight, Operation Space Power, Operation Space Power II
and other Cosmic activities, will continue for hundreds of years
into the future in order to balance the Karmic deficit caused by
what can only be bluntly described as the ignorance of
mankind. How intelligent is it really to use your most prominent scientific brains to develop a piece of equipment that can
destroy the whole world? To an alien race this is a form of
insanity. The Cosmic Missions of The Aetherius Society are
being, and will continue to be used to counterbalance madness
such as this. By joining an organization like The Aetherius
Society, no matter what role you play in it, you are contributing
to this life-saving work.

THE FIVE TEMPLES OF GOD
The Master Aetherius summed up the future role of The
Aetherius Society in another Cosmic Transmission entitled,
"The Five Temples of God," on August 26th, 1967. The fol-
lowing is a short extract from this Cosmic Transmission which
is published in full in a book of the same name:

*"You will experience many blows. You will experi-
ence many triumphs. You will have to be able to
drink the gall of defeat in the same balanced way
that you must drink the sweetness of triumph! You*

will be trained and tested in the fires of adversity. You will be further trained and tested by the subtle temptations of complacent victory, and you will be weeded and moulded, so that, eventually, those who are left will be worthy indeed for the great and majestic tasks which are to come.

"From this you can see that We have chosen The Aetherius Society for a great task. A task BEYOND that which We will give to any other organization upon Terra! Whether this task succeeds or fails is up to you. If it does fail, then you fail mankind and your Karmic Gods. If it does succeed, then quickly, ladies and gentlemen, not easily but quickly, will you be able to don the crowns of Adeptship—and even more resplendent crowns than that."

This advice was not just given for the Society now, but for the next thousand years at least. The Cosmic Masters Who contacted Dr. George King, contacted him with a task for the future, not just his lifetime, and in this extract the Master Aetherius gives some indication just how important to the world as a whole that future will be.

THE NEW AGE

In another Cosmic Transmission by the Master Aetherius entitled, "Become a Builder of the New Age," delivered on December 28th, 1963, He had already spelt out the serious implications of this coming New Age when He said:

"I think all of you know that only a small minority of men now living upon Terra will go into the New Age! The vast majority are not ready for it. If you know anything, you know that... You will be given the chance to prepare yourself to be one of the minority ready to go forward as the builders of the

New Age, or you will be a failure and join the com-
fort-loving, Truth-shirking masses...

"You should recognize this as a chance to prove
yourselves. Because, My friends, you will be given
this chance and it will be up to you whether you
take or leave it. You will always be allowed to exer-
cise your so-called freewill. You can choose whether
or not you will suffer limitation, or whether you will
start training now to be a builder of the New Age...

"Choose whether you will be one of the masses or
one of the builders. If you are one of the masses,
you will be reborn upon another, younger world and
there, I might tell you, you will have a much more
difficult job than building the New Age on your
Earth."

Years before this Transmission was delivered, the Cosmic
Masters had revealed through Dr. George King that another
Planet already exists in this Solar System, and that those members of the human race who do not change in the light of the
quickening vibrations as the New Age starts to dawn will go
there to continue their evolutionary process. It was made
absolutely clear that this is not a threat or a punishment, but
because those people would have proved that they were not
capable of living in the heightened vibrations coming to this
Earth. However, it would also be a missed opportunity of colossal proportions.

The ionosphere around us will gradually start to be removed.
It was no surprise to The Aetherius Society that an increased
ultraviolet ray bombardment has been detected and that holes
in the ozone layer have been discovered. Both these things
were foreshadowed by warnings that the ionosphere would be
taken down to allow increased Cosmic ray bombardment.
Indeed, warnings about holes in the ionosphere were specifically given in early Cosmic contacts with Dr. George King.

This process will take place gradually. It will not be an abrupt move but one which ensures that everyone has the fullest opportunity to make the necessary change and so earn their rightful place in the New Age. But you do not have to be an advanced Master to see that many people on this Earth disregard basic humanitarianism, never mind Spiritual Truth. Such people would be no more at home in a heavenly New Age on Earth than would a small child be at home in an advanced seminar at Harvard or Oxford Universities. The whole purpose of life is to gain experience, which, according to the Master Jesus in the Fourth Blessing, is "the greatest gift from man—or even God—to man." The Great Lords Who ensure that the Law of Karma works perfectly for the benefit of all life throughout the Universe know what conditions we need. It is for us at this time to prove that we are ready for the New Age so that we can inherit the positive Spiritual changes which are due to come to our world. If we do not, no matter who we are, what race, religion or culture we come from, we will go to this new Planet elsewhere in the Solar System to continue our evolutionary process.

THE COMING OF THE NEXT MASTER

Prior to this sorting of the wheat from the chaff, there will be another Coming. This will be the great Avatar prophesied by so many religious movements through the ages. St. Luke, Chapter 21, Verses 25-28, report Jesus as saying:

"And there shall be signs in the Sun, and in the moon, and in the Stars; and upon the Earth distress of nations, with perplexity; the sea and the waves roaring; men's hearts failing them for fear, and for looking after those things which are coming on the Earth: for the powers of heaven shall be shaken.

"And then shall they see the Son of man coming in

**a cloud with power and great glory. And when these
things begin to come to pass, then look up, and lift
up your heads; for your redemption draweth nigh."**

Not only does this fit in with other prophecies which speak of
a time of tribulation and cataclysm just prior to a Coming which
heralds a new Golden Era, it also reveals that the Son of man
will come in a cloud—which, as mentioned earlier, is Biblical
terminology for a UFO.

In 16th century France, one of the most famous prophets of
all time, Nostradamus, devised his codified system of quatrains
which predicted coming events. Possibly to protect himself,
Nostradamus wrapped up these prophecies in symbolic terminology, causing a multitude of interpretations to pour forth over
the centuries. On the whole they are much easier to understand
after the events than before them. He spoke of a period approximately 500 years after his lifetime when affliction would set in
around the Earth.

One of Nostradamus's most specific quatrains was no. 10.72.
It reads as follows:

**"In the year 1999 in the seventh month, a great
and terrible Lord will come from the sky, reviving the
great King of the Mongols—before and after his coming Mars will reign happily."**

This has been interpreted in many ways, but here is another
one. Situated in the ethers above the Gobi Desert, which is in
Mongolia, is a heavenly abode known to mystics throughout
the ages as Shamballa. The "King" of this etheric location is
known as the Kumara of Shamballa and He is responsible for
the higher Spiritual realms of this Earth. He has had to stand
back through the centuries from intervening in the affairs of
this physical world, due to the Karma of mankind. When the
next Master comes—and "terrible" in this context would mean

"awesome"—His Spiritual influence, and with it the power of the Masters of Earth, will be revived throughout the Earth. The influence of Mars, particularly through Satellite No. 3 which is controlled by Mars Sector 6, will be predominant around Earth before and after this time.

In one of his most important contacts with the Gods from Space, Dr. King received direct information about this great Coming. On November 23rd, 1958, during the charging of the Holy Mountain Brown Willy in Cornwall, as part of Operation Starlight, Dr. King received a Declaration from a Lord of Karma. This was not received while he was in a state of Samadhic trance, as the Cosmic Transmissions are received. It was an audible, powerful voice which he physically heard, just as Moses had heard the Voice of the Lord on Mount Sinai thousands of years earlier.

The following is an exact transcription of these words which are now known as The Lord's Declaration:

"There will shortly come Another among you. He will stand tall among men with a shining countenance. This One will be attired in a single garment of the type now known to you. His shoes will be soft-topped, yet not made of the skin of animals.

"He will approach the Earth leaders. They will ask of Him, His credentials. He will produce these. His magic will be greater than any upon the Earth — greater than the combined materialistic might of all the armies. And they who heed not His words, shall be removed from the Earth.

"This Rock is now Holy—and will remain so for as long as the world exists.

"Go ye forth and spread My Word throughout the world, so that all men of pure heart may prepare for His Coming."

This Declaration describes the Coming of an Interplanetary Master openly to Earth. The *"single garment of the type now known to you"* is the spacesuit so commonly described by those who have had close encounters with extraterrestrial Beings. These are seamless, one-piece suits which are often described as silver in colour. He will come in a Spacecraft and walk openly among mankind. Unlike previous Interplanetary Masters Who have visited this Earth, such as Sri Krishna, the Lord Buddha, the Master Jesus and others, He will not be born through the womb of an Earth woman, but will come in His Full Aspect, or unlimited Being. As the Lord's Declaration indicates, He will demonstrate His power, which previous Masters before Him have not been allowed to do by the Karmic Law which governs our world. When the Next Master comes, because His Coming will precede the final sorting of the wheat from the chaff—i.e. those who are going to inherit the New Age and become its builders, and those who have proved themselves not ready to remain on this Earth and will therefore go to the new Planet in this Solar System—this Master will be allowed to use His powers openly. This will be the final demonstration and there will be no doubt of His authority. He will have greater might, according to this Declaration, than all the armies on Earth.

"They who heed not His words, shall be removed from the Earth," applies to those who, even at this late stage, having had the ultimate demonstration of an Interplanetary Master with full powers, still do not listen, cooperate or change. They will then go to the new Planet. Many say they would like extraterrestrial Beings to land openly among us and prove themselves beyond all doubt. They do not realize that with such a landing would go a responsibility and a message they may not initially like. It would be a time of test as well as opportunity. All excuse for doubt would then be removed and people would have the choice of whether or not to cooperate with the Intelligences

who landed.

The Lord's Declaration closes with a Commandment: ***"Go ye forth and spread My Word throughout the world,"*** in order to give as much of mankind as possible the chance to change. As Pascal said: "Fortune favours the prepared mind." It is vital that as many people as possible take the opportunity to prepare themselves for this great change and to start now.

THE GREAT CHANGE

People sometimes say that they would love to believe in UFO's if only it was proven to them. Is this really true? Some psychologists believe that if a UFO landed in Washington, it would cause quite a stir for a few months and then people would become apathetic to it and walk around it on their way to work or some other mundane pursuit. This is surely the acid test. Will people really change when life on other Planets is proved to them beyond all doubt? There is a wealth of evidence of UFO activity already, and yet how many people are truly questioning the significance of this phenomenon? And would those who are, be willing to change their lives if necessary as a result of it?

The work of The Aetherius Society is to bring as much positive change to our world as possible before the coming of the Next Master, so that when it does take place, as many people as possible are prepared to respond to it. It may happen tomorrow, it may happen in a hundred years, or it may happen after that. But whenever it happens, only those who are ready will benefit—indeed, if it happens later, then more people will have the opportunity to be prepared for this event. Nostradamus gave the year 1999 and he may well have been right. But the whole purpose of prophecy is to try to change events for the better. All the outpouring of Spiritual Energy since Satellite No. 3 commenced its regular orbits in 1955, just to name one factor, may have postponed the date of this Coming to give more people the opportunity to change prior to the final sorting.

It is important to remember amid some of the prophecies of doom and gloom that the great change is essentially a wonderful thing for the Earth and all who choose to remain here, heralding a true Golden Era. The Master Aetherius described some of the changes which will come in a Cosmic Transmission delivered on June 1st, 1960, entitled "The New World":

"Gradually, mankind in the New World will learn to tap the great all-pervasive energy radiating from the Logos of the Planet as an Intelligence. He will be able to bathe himself in this great Light and thereby preserve his physical structure throughout the centuries. He will learn how to cause procreation without physical contact. He will learn how to communicate with all the worlds. He will conquer Space. He will be taken to the far ends of the Galaxy. Many and varied will be his experiences. He will gradually spread throughout the whole of Space, finding out for himself its great mysteries, solving these mysteries, understanding and living by the Great Laws.

"In these days, he will be evolved above all war. All thoughts of materialistic gain will be foreign to him. He will be evolved above all known political systems. He will be evolved above the use of his petty freewill and he will be given the key to the great portal of total Freedom."

In a book like this we can only introduce the main concepts of Dr. George King's Contacts with the Gods from Space. There is a wealth of other information for further study. As Mars Sector 6 said on September 24th, 1961, in a Cosmic Transmission entitled "Action is Essential":

"In these days the pearls are cast. If you be wise, you will find them amid the dust of life's road and cherish them, rejecting all else."

Epilogue

The motto of The Aetherius Society is taken from the Third Freedom, delivered by Mars Sector 6 through Dr. George King on February 22nd, 1961. It is simply the following nine words: *"Service is the Jewel in the Rock of Attainment."* This one statement sums up the essence of The Aetherius Society and, indeed, New Age philosophy as a whole.

Service has never been a very popular doctrine on this Earth. Self-development is far more popular because, frankly, it can include an aspect of selfishness which is so embedded in the psychology of mankind. Selfless Service, on the face of it, is an unrewarding activity from a personal point of view. But in actuality nothing could be further from the truth. Through Service, especially in these critical days, Karma is manipulated in its most potent form. The more selfless the action, the more Karma is balanced. The more effective the outcome for others, the greater benefit to the server as well.

Through Service, because Karma is manipulated in such a potent manner, all other things will follow. The days when it was recommended by the Masters to retreat into the wilderness in forests, caves, monasteries and other remote locations, in order to find personal enlightenment without regard for others, have now gone. Enlightenment has not gone and never will, because it is the natural birthright of all people to evolve and enlighten themselves. But the method of attaining it has changed.

The reasons for this change are clear: the Initiation of Earth and the quickening of all vibrations as a result; the presence of potentially world-destroying nuclear technology; the coming Aquarian Age and all that implies. All these factors provide an urgency which calls for the most effective Service possible. Through giving such Service you will advance, develop, and become more enlightened and free of restrictions. Correct physical conduct is essential; correct mental conduct is even more essential; but correct Karmic conduct is the most essential of all. Correct Karmic conduct in these days, as opposed to a thousand years ago, is Service to others.

Some would say that Service should be given without any Spiritual beliefs, that it is only possible to help others through material contributions of various kinds: food, medicine, housing and so on. Some politicians who believe this, want religious spokesmen restricted to the area of personal morality alone. But the true morality in these days is not so much how you lead your private life, important though that is, as how much you are contributing to the benefit of the world as a whole. Material contributions are essential but they do not get to the root of the problem, and so they do not bring lasting change. You can feed a person through money but you cannot get rid of greed with money, and so you cannot get rid of poverty. You can, if you are financially powerful enough, even influence the outcome of a particular war, but you cannot remove hate and so wars will recur. Only one force will remove and transmute these negative energies and emotions, and that is Service motivated by Love. Then you send the Spiritual Energy that is needed and this gets to the root of the problem.

If you wish to help a sick person who is dying of a heart condition, but refuses to give up smoking, follows an unhealthy diet and completely refuses to take any physical exercise, you can give them the most expensive treatment on Earth, but they will sooner or later deteriorate again. If you inspire that person to change their lifestyle, to have a more positive approach to themselves and their condition, and to be so concerned about others that they want to become fitter and more active, then you may help them to remove the sickness permanently and completely. In a sense humanity is like that sick person. Material help is essential in war-torn, disease-ridden, poverty-stricken areas, but ultimately, the whole problem will be solved when the consciousness of humanity changes. Even the prophecies will be changed for the better. The only lasting way to change that consciousness is to transmute the greed, hate and selfishness with an outpouring of Spiritual Energy conditioned by Love.

Love is a much abused word. Love in its highest and purest Spiritual expression is above personality. It is a motivation to help all life, not only human life, but animal and even vegetable life as well. It is the force which causes people to want to serve others. To quote Mars Sector 6 from The Third Freedom:

"The greatest Yoga is—SERVICE.
"The greatest Religion is—SERVICE.
"The greatest act is that act done in—SERVICE.
"Kill possession. Transmute selfishness into SERVICE for others and your reward will come. Enlightenment, like the break of dawn upon the darkest night, will cast the shadows of this night before it.
"Serve—and you will become enlightened.
"Serve—and you will be practising true selfless Love.
"Serve—and the mighty power of Kundalini will rise in natural, unforced fashion and open the Chakra jewels in your higher bodies. In will pour inspiration and you will be standing on the verge of the Initiation into Adeptship.
"There are no words great enough to describe the wonder of—SERVICE."

The greatest living thing in our Solar System is the Sun. It is the epitome of constant Service being performed. It is a God-like Being. Not only were many of the ancients right to revere the Mother Earth, they were also right to worship the Sun. The Sun is the source of all life in this Solar System, for all the energies that we use to exist are sent by God, the ultimate Source of all Creation, through the Sun. The Sun has set the finest example we can ever hope to witness. We take it for granted that the Sun will rise and set on a daily basis, that it will continue to pour forth its superb radiance. At our present stage of evolution, we will never witness a higher example of Spiritual Service than this.

Two thousand years ago, the Master Jesus came to give a radical new Spiritual Teaching. He had developed within Himself the powers that had been demonstrated by Masters before Him, such as walking on water, healing, exorcism, the manifestation of food and so on. But His Teaching was concerned with loving your neighbour as yourself, with forgiveness and tolerance towards those you know and come into contact with. It was radical in that it was based on Love and Service, but on what you might describe as a localized human scale. He has returned in these days to give a Cosmic concept. A concept of global Service and even Cosmic Service; not only loving those you meet, whether you are attracted by them or not, but of sending out your love to Beings like the Earth, the Sun, and even greater aspects of God than this.

These are true Teachings for these days. By following them, you can forge a pathway to the New Age for yourself and help many others to do so as well. You are warmly invited to investigate our Teachings. If you wish to help your fellow man, you will do so through The Aetherius Society. If you wish to help the ecological balance of the Planet on which you live, you will do so through The Aetherius Society. If you wish to progress and advance into higher consciousness and greater enlightenment, you will do so through The Aetherius Society. If you wish to cooperate directly with the Gods from Space, you will do so now and in the future through The Aetherius Society.

In 1986, Richard Lawrence was with Dr. King in Arizona at the exact time that he received a contact with an Intelligence from Mars just hours before the nuclear accident in Chernobyl in the former Soviet Union. Dr. King was told to prepare for a catastrophe which was shortly due and to activate the Spiritual Energy Radiator in Los Angeles for a series of operations. These continued over several days until the world came to know about the accident which had occurred at the Chernobyl nuclear power station. These operations did not stop the accident—that would have been Divine Intervention which would have contravened the Karmic Law. But many have reported that it could and should have been far more catastrophic than it was. Some have described it as miraculous that it was not. We later found out that these operations commenced only four hours and 23 minutes before the accident.

This is one of hundreds of incidents which epitomizes what cooperation with the Cosmic Masters can do. The Book of Revelations, Chapter 8, Verses 10-11, states:

"And there fell a great Star from heaven burning as it were a lamp... And the name of the Star is called Wormwood: and the third part of the waters became Wormwood: and many men died of the waters, because they were made bitter."

According to one scholar the word "Chernobyl" translates as "Wormwood." If this is so it summarizes the work which has to be done in these days. It is good to understand the prophecies, but it is truly great to work to change them into something better.

Dr. King, through his Contacts with the Gods from Space, has offered us a way to do this. He has set a pattern which many in the future will want to follow. Even in his latter years, in very poor health, he is performing another Cosmic Mission, known as Operation Power Light, designed to help the world in direct cooperation with the Cosmic Masters. This Mission started in March 1993—an extremely dangerous time, when there were astrological predictions of calamity as a result of a conjunction between Neptune and Uranus. Since Operation Power Light, which is designed to bring World Healing and Upliftment, there have been unexpected peace moves in the Middle East, Ireland and Bosnia, just to name three developments. Our world is not a safe place, but 1995 saw the first Christmas for many years when no two nations were at war.

All too often the truly great among us are only recognized after their demise. Dr. King has received many distinguished honours in the latter portion of his life, including his chivalric knighthood and his ecclesiastical archbishopric. His work has not yet been recognized, however, by the world as a whole. It is not too late, providing his legacy continues through the Missions and Teachings of The Aetherius Society. That is the opportunity the Gods from Space have offered the people of Earth at this crucial time.

There are several ways of investigating something, but by far the best is to try it out and test the results for yourself. If it works in your life, then you will know for sure, regardless of what anyone else may say or believe.

The Cosmic Contacts which have been made with His Eminence Dr. George King in the latter half of the 20th century rank among the Spiritual revelations of the ages. They represent a definite pathway to the New Age and potentially, a turning point for the entire human race. In the words of Dr. King himself:

"Go towards God now—even a Saint cannot reclaim a wasted minute."

Afterword to the Second Edition

Following Dr. King's passing in 1997, The Aetherius Society has gone from strength to strength. The Cosmic Missions have been expanded on many fronts and we are now performing The Saturn Mission, Operation Sunbeam, Operation Space Power, Operation Space Power II and Operation Prayer Power very actively indeed. In particular, three more locations now have Spiritual Energy Radiators—Auckland in New Zealand, Barnsley in the U.K., and Royal Oak, Michigan in the U.S.A.—which has expanded our output of spiritual energy exponentially.

The Teachings of The Aetherius Society have spread to many areas they have not reached before. The intervention in Chernobyl, described in the Epilogue, was confirmed in 2002 when the Russian journal, Pravda, published a report confirming that hundreds of people had seen a UFO hovering above the nuclear plant, while the accident took place. It concluded that this UFO had brought the radiation level down by almost four times, which prevented a devastating nuclear blast. This led to media coverage about our Teachings including one three-hour radio interview which was syndicated to approximately 500 radio stations across the U.S.A.

Cutting-edge scientists have accepted the concept of a multi-dimensional universe and are exploring the possibility of life beyond the visible light spectrum which is, after all, only a fraction of the electro-magnetic spectrum in its entirety. It is now accepted by astrophysicists that only 4% of the matter in the cosmos is actually detectable, and that even in the visible universe it is likely that there are many planets which can sustain life as we know it. Undoubtedly in the coming years, there will be other radical changes to the so-called certainties of scientific thought.

Religious thinking is under attack from atheistic and neo-

Darwinian cheerleaders, but still the spiritual impulse is strong in many. Those who disdain all organised religions are left with only two alternatives: disorganised religion or no religion at all. Either of these options would have a cataclysmic effect upon the precarious karmic balance of our world.

So what is the answer? If you choose to investigate further what you have read, there are several ways you can do so. You can look at the quality and calibre of teachings which have been received through Dr. King as Primary Terrestrial Mental Channel. You can test them by putting them into practice—performing the Twelve Blessings, going to the Holy Mountains of the world, cooperating with Spiritual Pushes and so much more. You can look for evidence from the Russian atomic accidents in the Urals and Chernobyl and other documented examples. You can see whether you consider the case presented by the Cosmic Masters to be logical, not so much from the perspective of academic argument as of basic commonsense. Above all, you can apply your intuitive sense or inner voice, which is best tapped through the path of contemplation and meditation.

But there is one more thing. One final and very significant revelation, which could not be made in the first edition: the true origin and calibre of Dr. George King. In his lifetime this was known only to a few, but now it can be made public. Like Shri Krishna, the Lord Buddha, the Master Jesus and certain other outstanding spiritual figures in our history, Dr. King was not of this Earth. He was not only a Master of Yoga and an outstanding Medium in his own right, he was in fact a Cosmic Avatar. A controversial statement but I have no doubt a true one.

I will leave you to draw your own conclusions, but I hope you will agree that the Mission he performed, and which still continues through The Aetherius Society today, marks him out as being "out of this world". If so, you will appreciate why I regard being invited to be his co-author as the greatest honour which could be afforded to any writer. Hence, *Contacts With The Gods From Space* is the book I have contributed to, which will always be closest to my heart.

Dr. Richard Lawrence

Bibliography

Abrahamson, Charles
  The Holy Mountains of the World, The Aetherius Society,
  1994
Berlitz, Charles
  Doomsday 1999, A.D., Souvenir Press Ltd, 1981
Blavatsky, H.P.
  Two Books of the Stanzas of Dzyan, The Theosophical
  Publishing House, 1956
Carpenter, Sue
  Past Lives, Virgin Books, 1995
Cope Schellhorn, G.
  Extraterrestrials in Biblical Prophecy, Horus House Press,
  Inc., 1989
Davenport, Marc
  Visitors from Time, Greenleaf Publications, 1992
Halpern, Paul
  Cosmic Wormholes, Plume, 1993
Hancock, Graham
  Fingerprints of the Gods, William Heinemann Ltd., 1995
King, D.D.,Th.D., George
  Cosmic Voice, Volume No. 1, 1957
  Cosmic Voice, Volume No. 2, 1957
  The Twelve Blessings, 1958
  Cosmic Voice, Issue No. 23, 1960
  You Are Responsible!, 1961
  Cosmic Voice, Issue No. 25, 1961
  Wisdom of the Planets, 1962
  The Nine Freedoms, 1963
  Become a Builder of the New Age, 1964
  Join Your Ship, 1964
  The Day The Gods Came, 1965
  The Five Temples of God, 1967

You Too Can Heal, 1976
Operation Sunbeam—God's Magic In Action, 1979
Visit To The Logos Of Earth, 1986
Operation Space Power, 1987
Contact With A Lord Of Karma, 1989
All the above books by George King, D.D.,Th.D.,
are published by The Aetherius Society.
Leslie, Desmond & Adamski, George
Flying Saucers Have Landed, T. Werner Laurie Ltd., 1953
Lovelock, James
Gaia, Oxford University Press, 1979
Muck, Otto
The Secret of Atlantis, Times Books, 1976
Scott-Elliot, W.
Legends of Atlantis and Lost Lemuria, The Theosophical
Publishing House, 1990
Sitchin, Zecharia
Genesis Revisited, Avon Books, 1990
Skinner, Stephen
Millennium Prophecies, Virgin Books, 1994
Thompson, Richard L.
Alien Identities, Govardhan Hill Inc., 1993
The Holy Bible (King James Version)

*For further information about The Aetherius Society,
please contact:*

American Headquarters
6202 Afton Place
Hollywood
California 90028-8298
U.S.A.

European Headquarters
757 Fulham Road
Fulham
London SW6 5UU
England

Tel: (323) 465-9652
(323) 467-HEAL

Tel: (020) 7736-4187

Website: **www.aetherius.org**

Index